# AGENDA

## Ekphrastic Issue

# AGENDA

## CONTENTS

## INTERVIEW

## POEMS

## REVIEWS/ESSAYS

*Front cover painting*: 'After the Cheltenham Festival' by Frieda Hughes
*Back cover paintings*: 'An unquiet Mind' by Frieda Hughes and Frieda
                        Hughes with some of her 400 DAYS paintings

# Introduction by Patricia McCarthy

Welcome to this double 'Ekphrastic' issue of *Agenda*.

Ekphrasis, from the Greek, traditionally referred to a vivid, often dramatic, verbal description of a work of art. However, modern poets have mostly broadened the term and try to interpret, inhabit, confront and speak to their subjects. This issue of *Agenda* sees ekphrastic poetry as one art form being inspired by another, whether it be painting, sculpture, photography, film or music.

Many of us are familiar with ekphrastic poetry without necessarily defining it as such. Think of Keats 'Ode on a Grecian Urn', or Auden's 'Shield of Achilles'. Within these pages you will find many interesting poems, interviews, essays and reviews concerning this subject in all its variety, inspiration and skill.

The accomplished poet, Myra Schneider writes about how she is drawn to write ekphrastic poems:

> I have been thinking about why I often write ekphrastic poems,
> particularly poems about paintings, and I've come to the
> conclusion that it's for two reasons. The first is that I love colour.
> Wearing colourful clothes, having colourful things round me:
> cushions, duvet covers, bowls of fruit, flowers, all make me feel
> more alive. In winter when there is so much darkness I search out
> colour and light for comfort. The work of artists such as Matisse,
> Van Gogh, Chagall, Dufy, Cézanne, Bonnard, Turner and Hokusai,
> excites me and has offered starting points for poems in which I've
> explored different kinds of material. I first saw Bonnard's 'The
> Red Cupboard' in an exhibition and the painting seemed to pull
> me across the gallery floor. The poem it triggered questioned why
> we use images, explored a childhood memory and feelings the
> memory aroused.
>
> Secondly, I've noticed that the visual plays a prominent role in
> my poems and that a starting point for me is frequently something
> I've seen. It might be a painting or a sculpture but it might be an
> object in the house: light catching on a bottle, plastic packaging I
> couldn't remove or something I've seen outside: a postbox with its
> opening blocked at the time of a postal strike, a lopped tree trunk,
> a small incident I've witnessed in the park behind our house or on
> a train. I write long narrative poems and these too often include
> strongly visual scenes or details which connect with narrative or
> move it on: a woman experiencing a sense of revelation as she

looks at an advertisement in a station, a key character shocked when he sees his reflection in a stream because his appearance is very different from the image he has of himself. It seems that my thinking process, my exploration of feelings, ideas and contemporary issues is anchored to seeing and that this is why I write ekphrastic poems.

Myra's pamphlet, *Five Views of Mount Fuji* (Fisherrow Press, 2018, £5), proceeds from the sale of which go towards The Grenfell Foundation, illustrates beautifully how her poems and the prints of Katsushika Hokusai (1760-1849) partner each other. One poem, 'Measuring the Pine Tree', demonstrates how ekphrastic poetry can evolve, with the poet here becoming 'one of the three// trying to measure the tree's massive girth/ by stretching arms right around the bole'. In another poem, 'River', the 'unmanned craft/visible through the tall piers' in the print metamorphosise into 'benign creatures basking'.

This brings me to recommend a beautiful book permeated with the essence of a nostalgic rural Englishness: song-writer Virginia Astley's *The English River: a journey down the Thames in poems and photographs* (Bloodaxe Books, 2018, £12). As Gillian Clarke says in the blurb: 'the pictures show the way, while the poems have their own imagery, their own music, and lines that linger in the mind'.

Two more really beautiful books in the hand worth mentioning are: *Achill The Island*, poems by John F Deane and paintings by John Behan (Currach Press, 2018, hardback). Just as in *The English River*, the paintings, magically coloured and executed, breathe out the very air and spirit of Achill's wild landscape and traditions, and go hand-in-hand with John F Deane's remarkable poems inspired by his beloved childhood island.

The other book, a hardback also, has to be *Morning, Paramin*, by Derek Walcott, artwork by Peter Doig (Faber & Faber, 2016, £22). Here is another wonderful collaboration between Nobel-prize-winning Walcott from St Lucia and multi award-winning Peter Doig, a Scottish painter living in Trinidad since 2002. Here – unlike the previous book, where Ireland's leading sculptor John Behan's paintings respond to the poems – Walcott's poems respond to the paintings. Poignantly, this book came out in November, 2016, just four months before Walcott's death on March 17, 2017 (*Agenda*'s special issue on Derek Walcott, guest edited by Maria Cristina Fumagalli, Vol 39, Nos 1-3, 416pp, came out in the winter of 2002-3 – some copies still available).

Not wanting to leave out a couple of other books saved for this topic, it is worth having a close look at *Milking the Sun: ag Crú na Gréine*: the

Irish of Seán O'Ríordáin translated by Gabriel Fitzmaurice (both poets of considerable stature) accompanied by stunning, almost primitive paintings by Brenda Fitzmaurice (Salmon Poetry, 2018), and also *Luck is the Hook*, by Imtiaz Dharker whose poems, at her unforced best, are memorable and whose own black and white drawings, twenty-three in number, evolve to interweave successfully her handwritten text with some drawings.

Dylan Willoughby's beautifully produced book, *Les Festivals des Murmures* (1918), with Letterpress printing, typesetting and binding by Robert Walp at Chester Creek Press in the village of Chestertown, New York, consists of twenty numbered and signed copies set by hand in Eric Gill's Perpetua type and printed on a variety of hand and mould made papers: Kitakata, Canson Ingres, Chester Creek Handmade Gray, Somerset Book. The papers, many with ragged edges, are in a mixture of shades and thicknesses – brown-paper brown, slate, mauve, grey, dark cream, lighter cream and so on. The pages are un-numbered and the twenty-two poems are illustrated by Anthony Mastranatteo. The squirls in different shades weave around and under the poems, and the figures, geometric shapes and patterns complement the poems beautifully. The haunting poems revolve around lost love, ghosts, souls, myths and there are many memorable lines, a few examples of which are:

What are we but the sum of our lost tenses?

…rain the outpouring of lost souls

Come closer than I am to myself

Your touch is a calling I did not know

…who are we but flight

This little book, hard-backed, is a work of art in itself, and maybe this is the way poetry volumes should be heading in our age of mass production and cheap print-outs.

Time, now, for the contents, ekphrastic and otherwise, in the following pages, to speak for themselves.

# Carol Rumens

## Stabat Mater *(after Pergolesi)*

*Stabat mater dolorosa*
*Juxta crucem lachrimosa…*

The downed tools of the trees   non-running water   power
off   the wind a trickle      adrenaline zero
he bled for 3 days   she throws the veil over her eyes

long sandswept lament      across the desert
entering      like the sepsis stony priests
bring with their blessing      pharaonic circumcision
to the doors of the vulgate   to the key of F minor

*No-one factored in a wept-for daughter*
*god-not-the-father   how at the menarche's terror*
*I washed her by hand   hung smalls to whiten branches*

*her blood was hard to wash out*
                                                *there was a sword*
*planted in her   the sword of our mutilation*

She throws the veil over her eyes

she touches the cross   she meets its fissured stem
at the cross between her thighs   bark and dry splinters
(she bled for 3 days)   the cut-down rose is only
the sum of its weapons   sharper for want of sap

*We're thorned by suffering   genital-gardened   stuck*
*with nails and sticky with rusted blood   recaptured if we run*
*resurrect      resurrect us all*

she tells her girl on the wing   her scarlet-feathered
phoenix filia in the gathering wind
*let's not in love or hatred live like icons.*

*We gave what we could. Those who are the most gifted*
*are sometimes leafless trees   some of their children hang there*

# Peter Carpenter

## Homage to Bill Brandt

*Nude, East Sussex, April 1953*

You would live with the giantess
like a cat at her feet.
She has been left here to meet
the incoming tide. Face down
on gradations of shingle,
a dark tress of hair flops
across her hips. Towards us
the curve of her arse
is the underbelly of a Supermarine
Swift, the slope in Westbury
where that White Horse
is carved in chalk.

Face down, her nostrils
twitch at flecks of sea-spray
that mottle her back.
The cliffs here at Seaford
are the sandwiched evidence
of what was, millions
of years tucked into the brief
as part of the case for the defence.

When she steps away
there are indentations
down her front. They turn her
for a moment into a Seurat
*poseuse en profil*
circa 1886. You mutter
'voluptuous' and proffer
the beach towel,
its warmth, its whiteness,
its terrycloth ridges.

# Julia Deakin

## It has rained

and the blackberries you thought you'd miss
have sucked up the soaked earth to party one more week
around the snickets, building sites and lay-bys.
Behind allotment borders they cavort in parody
of garden soft fruits – shoot through cracks, prize walls apart
and manufacture vitamin-grenades free for the plucking.
Shouldn't such luck be suspect? If not poisonous, then
licensed? Yet there's enough for every thief and then some

always just beyond reach, tempting you to fall headlong
into that ditch-trickery. Hand over fist their promise loops
and spools, tangles and lures you down September lanes,
away from the learning world to where the untutored hedge
sets out its stall: its blood from stones, its wine
from rainwater, its alchemy.

# The Draw-well Walk

In those days when you had to walk to water and work,
paths went from A to B the shortest way to save Shanks's pony.
So though they called the Draw-well Walk the Wynde
it didn't – it ran quite straight along the backs of houses
between walls too high to see into the plots behind
(except occasionally, through the cracks of latched wooden gates)
from those lesser streets to out beside the Market Hall
on High Street opposite Wycherley's.

Only sometimes in the quiet between those walls
there drifted, as if in consolation for things unseen
that not-quite woodsmoke smell – yesterday's bonfires
perhaps, crumbling mortar, foxes, bricks or a mix of them all –
which though you weren't yet ten took you back a century
to the middle of eighteen-sixty-five, where you stood
forgetting your errand as you breathed instead that faint tang
that took you another century back, on a path
straight to the past.

# Robert Stein

## Stanley Spencer in Saxby St., Leeds, 1949

It is Tuesday, it is Wednesday, it is no time at all.
The grey paving stones will resurrect soon and be carried as shields.
The bus will stop, judder and burst its heart. It is not rain
it is revelation; shop shutters are wings,
fruit of temptation greengrocers grow
and their vegetables sprout,
self-peel and uncoil,
ladder to the next day,
the shore, the sky, the holiday.

And this butcher, and this baker who leans out
all the day to chat proud, shipcrest friendly,
sees a boy carrying a sword, a woman with a bowl
who are rooted by the land though they strain to leave the earth,
have the accent of the town but would speak in other tongues
are gesturing with handkerchiefs in frantic friendship
are shaking two hundred white surrender handkerchiefs
bidding themselves goodbye, aloft to give their all.

# Marek Urbanowicz

## Sketch for Henryk Kuna*

This room has one window.
The walls are pictureless,
the floor laid with frayed rugs.
Old newspapers muffle
his stiff shuffle and tread.

The skylight's grime lets in
the ghosts of the city:
snatches of speech, Polish,
German; a soldier's step
gooses his bone-white skin.

He gauges the seasons
by flights of geese. His meals
come with a coded knock,
with a rare cigarette.
He sends back black faeces.

For days he can stare at
the sky's clouded canvas;
better this than ghettoed,
his friends yellow-banded
then freighted to the camps.

He draws the odd charcoal
never paints but has placed,
where the thin-fingered light
gleams longest, a child's bust
without arms, legs, torso.

Each day he shapes the face,
sculpts ears, nose, rounds a mouth
out of his own dumbness
to voice across the red
parted seas, past broken,

war-torn seasons to sing,
wordless but clear tongued, through
shaped clay to the grandson
who claims and writes this room,
whose child sketches a face.

*Henryk Kuna (1879-1945).

'One of the outstanding Polish sculptors of the first half of
the 20th Century... during the German occupation he was
in hiding near Warsaw, creating a few sculptures and drawing.'

# David Pollard

## Paula Modersohn-Becker (1876-1907)

*On Her Sixth Wedding Day,* 1906 tempera on canvas,
Paula Modersohn-Becker Museum, Bremen

Oh how I seem
and seeming, image out my own retreat
from the eye's penetration of lost love,
how the frail skin is only mineral oils
almost as thin as life and love
whose quiet half smile
can colour me this game of lies.

My only signed and dated –
so you can tempt out the truth
from this *cadavre exquis*
of marriage and the expectancy
and rose of my fertility
and of art's betrayals
– my belly's contour –
lifelines read as destiny
and paint.

# Matisse

1906, Royal Museum of Fine Arts, Copenhagen

*I quickly sense any disaccord between my hand the 'je ne sais quoi' in*
*myself which seems submissive to it.*

Matisse

And so it all makes sense –
He played the violin.
His harmonies: the double and quadruple stopping
sing together in the clarity of timbre.

And so the thing translated into
the ambiguities of space,
the chords of many colours
their clashes harmonized in
the polyphony of his two dimensions.

Bleeding his colours from some other source
than what he saw, abstracted as
his eyes created signs of spatiality
and the quick cut of time in stark.

And finally the eyes too large and deep
to sound the patina of seeing yet grasp
the blaze of life onto the unfinished
finality of what he knew.

# Siân Thomas

## Moth Line

*After Van Gogh's* 'Poppies and Butterflies'

'Lovely, tell your mother.'
My grandma's voice echoes through my mother.
Their language hovers like an aura or a layer,
one woman upon another, pressed like the flowers
in the gardening book my mother gave me,
like the oriental poppies I lay between the sheets,
bright as butterfly wings.

My childhood garden echoes through the plants
I nurture now: poppies, honesty, forget-me-nots,
lines of memory, true lines, lost lines.
My grandma sitting on the bench by our back door
picking redcurrants while butterflies swarm around
the buddleia like they haven't swarmed in years.

Her long nose like mine, our strong sense of smell,
always pressing our faces into flowers.
I'm the last woman in our line and no mother,
no ripe seeds to offer. In a week or two the honesty
will be out with its scent like honeyed pepper
and I'll spend my evenings hovering, inhaling.

This year I'll say aloud to the garden,
'Lovely, tell your mother.'
My grandma might be with me as a moth:
white wings for hair,
blue eyes morphed to wing spots,
floral talcum powder, long nose, tongue.

The women in my family are lepidoptera:
after death my mother and I will hang
from petal edges, unroll our tubular tongues,
feed on sugar-water, crushed redcurrants,
sticky fingers of our human lives;
the line of spirits folded, wings pressed
like petals between pages.

# Caroline Maldonado

*These poems are from a sequence 'The Creek Men' written in response to the sculptures of Laurence Edwards to be found in the East Anglian landscape.*

## Ever Rooted

The hawk on a weathervane
by the replica bridge turns
its head from side to side.

It looks real. I stand quite still.

A pregnant sheep, her legs
pointing crookedly up,
struggles to get right but can't.

A pike, two foot long,
lies with open jaw, killer fangs
and black holes, eyes sucked dry.

The creek men aren't dead.
They're rooted and ready.

One presses against the wind.
Another leans on his branch
to hold up. He looks like mud.

# Borders

That man's borders are menaced.
He can feel it in the wire and sticks
that are his bones.

He will defend what's his
with all he's got,
with every thistle, every clod.

The horizon, split by mist,
streams towards him
and he's posed to meet

the marauders head-on
but he himself is beyond the pale.
He's of the marshlands.

With that mashed-up face
you can tell
he's not one of us.

# Out of Place

The bandages binding his calves
flap round his ankles. He strides on,
white with dust, has places to go,
far from the marshlands.

He hitches
a ride, a lorry stops, he sits up beside
the driver and from there he sees
the motorway split in two,
its lanes vanishing into trees,
out of time.

The man won't look back.
Heading for the city, he has work to do.
He'll be dropped off in a place
he may have known once

and dreamed of returning to,
now a dry land of crowded crossroads
where silence is gone and neon lights
are too strong for his deep-scored eyes.

One day in a station's dim corner
you'll come across him, a heap,
his crooked branch-arm stretched out.

# Wendy Holborow

## The Dance

*The Cha Ca Cha that was Danced in the Early Hours of 24th March, 1961.*
*A Painting by David Hockney.*

I didn't know you back in '61
perhaps
things would have been different –
childhood sweethearts –
two red he(art)s instead of the br(own) upon black

black for you who cheated,
brown for me the conspirator
conscripted to      y(our) love

your name worn on my sleeve
not on my upper thigh
        as we dance – not the cha cha
cha,
  but ensconced
in each other's arms
gentle together
        your voice wrapped around me

aware of the warped jealousy
of other women wanting      you
       only have e(yes) for me
I love every mo(ve)ment
quavers dance across my neck

# Richard Ormrod

## Autumn in the Aude

*(For S)*

After Van Gogh's 'Harvest at La Crau'

'Life can only be understood backwards, but it must be lived forwards.'
Kierkegaard.

They have dead-headed the sunflowers now---
threshed and thrashed them to bare brown bones,
sticks of broom—squeezed their seeds' life-blood
for oil—left them bereft of all their beauty,
dignity and pride: row on row, a battleground
after mass-slaughter, field upon field
upon field...a faint glow (or is it an illusion?)
seems to hover over them like a ghostly
presence, their essence departed...

Symbolic, perhaps, of all our autumns---
seasons, treasons, reasons, all dead-headed,
discarded; dreams squeezed dry—lost,
tossed in the quick-lime of time,
irrevocable; and yet...a stray glint of gold
clinging on, limpet-like, recalls how
these stalks are ploughed back in
to enrich the soil for next year's crop,
year upon year, upon year...

Immortality...

# Merryn MacCarthy

*(Inspired by a painting by Yamazaki Joryu,*
*'Courtesan reading a letter beside a mosquito net')*

## Kimono

Transparencies of blue
mosquito nets.
I enter a small French garden
as from time past,
joyful anticipation
beyond winter's cocoon.

They hang within,
this artist's collection,
her hair, her passion flaming.
 She shows me rustic kimonos
woven from natural plants,
leaf, grass, stem, bark.

She guides me through
their calligraphy
with Ariadne's thread.

Japan, the very name
for me forbidden.
My mother forced to flee
from China, a musical box
never to be played.
The kamikaze pilots

of my father's war,
Hiroshima, Nagasaki,
the only names I knew.
Friends tortured,
starved in prison camps.
All was fearful, ablaze.

Yet it is 'Madam Butterfly'
I now recall,
women delicate, skilled,
kimonos flickering, floating
out of the blue
to lighten my load.

I burst forth robed
in corn-coloured chanvre,
hemp, wide-sleeved,
protected. Symbolic hope
of cancer overcome:
my coat of sun.

# Interview with Pascale Petit

**P McC**: As a well-known poet who started out as a sculptor, can you explain why you crossed over from one art form to another? For example, what drew you to sculpture in the first place? And then poetry? And was sculpture not enough for what you wanted fully to express?

**PP**: From the beginning I made art, sculptures and painting and drawings, and I wrote poems. Drawing came first, when I was six in school in Paris, as a means of escape into a world of my own, when I was a very withdrawn child. Then, when I was about fifteen I discovered Keats and the rest of the Romantics, in school, and realised whatever poetry was was what I wanted to do. But I also needed to be a visual artist, to make a world of my own. For the first few decades of my life I was torn between the two art forms. I didn't do them both together, because when I did one I did it obsessively, full time, and wasn't even interested in the other. That would continue for a year maybe, then I'd switch.

I would guess my withdrawal from sculpture started when I went to the Royal College of Art to do my MA in sculpture, when I was thirty two. I had a tough time there; sculpture was hard for women then, and one male tutor (they were all male) in particular objected to my feminism. Perhaps because I felt I had to prove myself against the male standard and strength, I would set myself technically challenging projects, using toxic materials like resin and fibreglass, labour intensive pieces, requiring unpleasant processes like using a grinderette for days on end.

I've since discovered quite a few sculptors / installation artists, who were working then, who might have influenced me to work in a more pleasurable way. But I didn't know about them, and felt that I had to measure up to the monumental style male standard, and that I couldn't. What's more, I was never interested in that kind of work – in formal sculptural elements, aesthetics as such. But it was all we were taught. If only I'd known about Annette Messager, for example, or Mark Dion, or Louise Bourgeois – work about life, family, natural history. But we were not exposed to those kinds of artists, only to the more monumental male ones, such as Henry Moore.

One day a good friend of mine called at home and I was sanding the stairs with my small old sanding machine and it was taking days to do one step, when he said what I was doing was masochistic, that I should just paint the stairs. So I did. And I thought about my art practice and realised that too was not good for me. I had a long think about it and decided to stop! But that was a big decision because it was what I had always lived for.

*Rainforest Art* at the Natural History Museum 1990, Pascale with her work.
photo Richard Watt.

Poetry in contrast seemed harder to do (because I wasn't very good at it), but didn't involve hurting myself. I could make metaphors and images without having to grapple with materials and processes such as resin casting, aluminium casting, glass blowing / plaster moulding. I didn't write good poems for a long time; back then there were no courses or workshops and I didn't have a mentor. I am completely self-taught, having spent six years at art school but studied no poetry beyond 'A' level.

**P McC**: Which sculptors, and visual artists, have most influenced you? And, in turn, which poets?

**PP**: When I was a sculptor, the only sculptor that influenced me was Joseph Cornell. I loved his glass boxes, and I made glass boxes on a large scale, two whole interlinked structures of them, with natural history objects inside, torn photographs of my family, thorns, nests, stuffed birds, beetles. The Natural History Museum in London used to give me specimens. The first glass structure was called 'Ancestral Memory' and the second 'Bodytrap'. Both were about my birth and much else. I was trying to put entire rainforests and coral reefs in them. One of the Visiting Fellows told me about Frida Kahlo when I was at the RCA, but I didn't get into her deeply as an influence then, because she was a painter. I wish I had! She has since been a huge influence, especially her imagery and use of thorns, animals, and female portraits.

Now, as a poet, I am influenced by a vast array of visual artists, am constantly on the lookout for new influences. They are at least as important as poets to my writing. The art that influenced my last book *Mama Amazonica*, for instance, ranges from Walton Ford's animal paintings, to Anselm Kiefer's flower paintings, from Julien Salop's sculptures of web-entangled deer, virtually every taxidermy artist, and Raw Art.

For my next book, with the working title of *Tiger Girl*, current artists I'm drawing from are Mark Dion, the Chinese firework artist Cai Guo-Qiang, and Henri Rousseau. I surround myself with big books of their art, and watch films of Cai's installations. I'm also very keen on Bill Viola, I'll travel far to see new works by him.

Poets who have influenced me are Selima Hill, Sharon Olds, Ted Hughes, Ferenc Juhasz, C.K. Williams, Pablo Neruda, Joy Harjo. But there are far more that I read and love, and learn technically from, including Mark Doty, Les Murray, Yang Lian. Current favourites include Natalie Diaz and Traci Brimhall. There is nothing quite like discovering a new favourite!

**P McC**: It can easily be said that you now sculpt with words. Can you enlarge upon this?

*Ancestral Memory* Pascale Petit, photo Graham Bush.

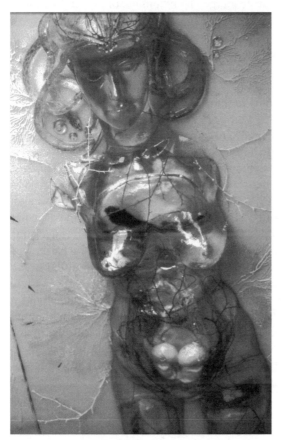

*Mirror* (detail) Pascale Petit 1984, casting resin, thorns, birds, beetles, acrylic paint.

*Pitcher Plant I* Pascale Petit 1990.

**PP**: Thank you for saying that. If I do, it's because I still need to make sculptures and installations, but with words, not materials. I like to think that my books are an exhibition with some poems made into sculptures and others into installations to walk inside. I do need the works to be as physical as possible, to create images in the reader's mind, a world real enough to help me (and hopefully them) to survive.

**P McC**: In your collections you curate your images with a painter's eye. Paintings are at the heart of the poems, especially in your collection *What the Water Gave Me* where you focus on the paintings and life of Frida Kahlo, and at the same time are inspired by Remedios Varo and Franz Marc. Can you describe how you manage to blur the distinctions between the art forms where poetry, painting and music merge? I am thinking of two of your lines, though there are of course many:

> I longed for harmonies to grow the trees
> so the songs of their light would flood my studio.

**PP**: I must confess that I know nothing about music as an art. I don't even listen to music much, preferring birdsong. Though I think birdsong is music. My favourite resource is Xeno Canto https://www.xeno-canto.org/ where I can listen to the songs of any bird around the world, and there are plenty in my garden. The music I describe is often natural, made by trees, animals, birds. But then there is the music of the spheres. I have read a number of books about that, such as *The Mystery of the Seven Vowels* by Joscelyn Godwin. I also have a lot of books about ethnographic music, in particular music made by the Warao of the Orinoco Delta, the *icaros* – or curing chants – of the shamans of the Peruvian Amazon, So I am fascinated by harmonics and the relationship of sound, poetry, and stars, and I'm interested in the Navajo Beauty Way and Dawn chants.

Many Amazonian tribes know that song has colours, perfumes and a physical form. The Desana tribe of Brazil have an extensive mythology about this, how every being in the forest has a corresponding harmony, smell and colour, and that these correspond to shapes and perceptions in the brain. I don't knowingly try to blur the different senses or art forms, but hope that a hint of my researches comes through.

**P McC**: In this blurring of art forms, some of your poems are full of visions, for example your vision of Europe devastated by the First World War, linked to Franz Marc's paintings, with archetypal horses moving in the wastes. Here, 'at the edge of the trenches'

... a red mare is giving birth
to a white colt with wings soft as drifts.

The 'wings soft as drifts' immediately conjure a visionary experience. Do these kind of experiences happen consciously to you, and are they linked to any kind of spirituality?

**PP**: The lines come from images in my head, and in this case the images came from Franz Marc's paintings, which have a primitive lyrical quality, held in the innocent form of horses, which have an extra poignancy because they were used in battle, and Marc rode one as a despatch rider.

I am spiritual in that I believe we are more than physical beings, and that good and evil are played out through us. I was brought up as a Catholic, but I'm an animist now. I think animals and trees have souls.

**P McC**: I agree with you. I am sure they have. Have you inherited your grandmother's second sight?

**PP**: Only a touch. I have had supernatural experiences, out-of-the-body waking dreams, and I get déja vu – I expect we all have that. But she had second sight and she said it was a burden to her. She knew when a neighbour died, and would see their ghosts. When I lived with her as a child she used to dress up in gypsy clothes and tell fortunes at fairs – this was in mid-Wales. She kept her gypsy clothes in the coal-house in a box, and I loved to rummage through it and try them on. She was born in Rajasthan, and half Indian, but I didn't know that then, as it was a family secret that she was the baby of her father's maid.

**P McC**: In the Frida Kahlo poems, you give her a voice with her wounds, re-inventing this woman who expressed her life through paint, with her theatrical, indigenous clothes that hid the broken body beneath. Did you almost become Frida in the writing of these? And would you say that all the anatomical and gynaecological details, topped by the exotic ones, enabled you to translate your own pain into hers, since wounds recur through the corpus of your oeuvre, both personally and impersonally expressed?

**PP**: It was exciting to pretend to be Frida, and yes in some ways I stopped being me in the process, and put on her extravagant, extraverted persona, which was a release (I'm very introverted!). I only tried to become her so that I could paint my own equivalents of her paintings in words, though. Otherwise, I wouldn't dare! What led me to identify with her was when I

31

read Carlos Fuente's introduction to her extraordinary diary. Referring to the accident she suffered as a teenager, when a bus rail pierced her back and exited her vagina, he said that she was raped by a bus. I thought that here was a way for me to write about rape and childhood abuse without having a perpetrator to blame. She was wounded by a bus colliding into her streetcar. I could write about the shock and trauma of that, as a violent image, without even having to be personal. I was interested in the image and the fast movement of it, the theatre of it, not in the emotions so much.

It's true that much of my work concerns itself with trauma and transmitting pain, and how we deal with pain and suffering. I've had long periods of physical and mental illness and I think it's important to attempt to write about illness as it's so universal and part of being human.

**P McC**: When focusing on a particular painting as the source for a poem, do you stick to what you see in the painting, or do you let your imagination embellish it and maybe take off in different directions?

**PP**: My approaches vary. Sometimes I'm faithful to the painting and its story, and acknowledge my source, and sometimes I just use it as a springboard. Always, what I'm trying to do is write a poem that's as vital as the artwork, which is of course impossible, but worth a try! With Frida's painting 'What the Water Gave Me' I couldn't write about it at all for years, while trying to respond literally to it, to her lying in her bath surrounded by icons and scenes from her life. Once I took off from the painting, and imagined what happened after it – the ascension I describe – then I was away. Then I wrote five more poems about it, all different approaches, but only one stuck fairly closely to the details in the frame.

**P McC**: Can you tell us more about your use of masks in dealing with traumatic poems about your father in your strong collection *Fauverie* set in Paris, where you went to see, for the first time in decades, the father who had abandoned you aged eight? These masks themselves are like artefacts, with the jungle imagery and wild animals that you so cleverly twist in and through poems about abuse, and, in a way, make the ugly beautiful.

**PP**: Thank you for saying that, Patricia. The animal masks suddenly occurred to me, after visiting the Jardin des Plantes zoo. I'm much more interested in the animals and the flora of the rainforest than my father. But bringing a traumatic primary relationship into the natural history gives it intensity and immediacy for me. I'm writing about something crucially important to me, yet finding ways to describe tropical nature at its most intense.

32

**P McC**: You are very brave in your tackling of taboo subjects as you swing between pain, exposure of violence, and resurrection. How have you found readers reacting to the vibrant intensity of what you depict?

**PP**: It varies, some people like the vibrancy and extremes, and others shy away. Occasionally I get a reaction, usually from a man, and they'll say 'keep it to yourself' or, stop writing confessional/personal poems! I don't intend to do that. Violence towards women, children, and the natural world, is worldwide, and very extreme in some cultures. Just because it's polite to cover up in Britain, doesn't mean I have to oblige. In general I'd say my work tends to provoke either love (and approval) or distaste (and disapproval). Each book usually gets one review (usually by a man) disapproving of the personal approach of my work.

**P McC**: Has the sense of being an outsider given you a freedom to write what is pushed out of you? And is it deliberate: your ensuring that this does not come out too raw but is fashioned into a word-painting through your choice of backgrounds and colourful imagery?

**PP**: Because I didn't have a literary education, and am self-taught, and also because I'm not British (though I've recently acquired UK nationality because of Brexit), I do feel like an outsider. But I grew up feeling like an outsider, an alien, and so this feeling of not being quite like other children, and therefore humans, has affected how I write, and yes, given me the freedom to do what I want. There are penalties, such as the reviews/ responses I mentioned earlier, but I write what I am compelled to write.

I don't choose particular background settings, such as the Amazon, deliberately. It's more that I write about what excites me, and the Amazon, and nature at its extreme and wildest, does this. Maybe the human protagonists are the background and nature is the foreground?

**P McC**: All the wild animals and birds in your work too seem almost painted in or stitched into the tapestry of the poem. From where did you get this passion for animals both wild and tame?

**PP**: I'm not at all sure, but I'd guess I bonded with animals as a baby, when I came to live with my Indian/Welsh-Irish grandmother, and she had seven cats, a dog, a budgie, a rabbit, and her council house was in the middle of farm country. Perhaps because I was brought to her when I was two weeks old, taken from her when I was two years old, then sent back to Paris to my parents, moved for two years into a children's home, to stays with families in other countries, then sent back to my Gran in Wales, maybe this confused me, and I thought my mother was a cat! Or a comfort at least, when I had no stable mother figure to rely on.

**P McC**: How have your travels helped your poetry?

**PP**: My four trips to the Amazon basin are the biggest influence on my poetry. I went to the Venezuelan Lost World twice when I was forty two, then recently I went to the Peruvian Amazon, again twice. These travels changed my life and are the basis of my writing.

**P McC**: In your latest collection, *Mama Amazonica* (Bloodaxe, 2017), a Poetry Book Society Choice, you seem to have developed your technique in juxtaposing everyday details such as the medical ward and medical terms, with wonderful jungle images. To me, this juggling with the lyrical and the brutally real makes the poems all the more shockingly powerful and moving. Can you comment on this?

**PP**: Thank you, I'm glad you find it works. The thing about the Amazon rainforest is that it's both a stunningly beautiful place, but also dangerous and uncomfortable. The humidity alone is uncomfortable, as is the constant onslaught of biting insects. It is the unknown. The scientists at Tambopata Research Center, the lodge where I stayed that's the only lodge for guests in the whole Tambopata National Reserve, are doing a systematic log of all the new species they discover, and know there are many more. They are cataloguing them before they vanish. So the beauty and wonder of the place is counterbalanced by its vulnerability – it is in the process of disappearing. You could say it is sick and abused, like the mother in a psychiatric ward, who has a mental illness the doctors cannot diagnose. Although she is vulnerable, and indeed dies from over-medications, she is dangerous and unpredictable as the jungle.

**P McC**: In this mesmerising collection, you also have many ekphrastic poems inspired by a variety of artists. In what way do paintings of others support your poetic craft?

**PP**: I look to the visual arts to refresh my image bank. Visual artists, especially installation and video artists, are often bolder than poets, bolder than I am anyway. I look to them to help me make new connections between images, and I guess because I'm excited by their work and that in turn excites mine.

**P McC**: Again, in *Mama Amazonica*, the theme of abuse and violence is focused upon, from the heart of your own experience, and the images of the flora and fauna in the Amazon rainforest, so beautifully culled by you, contrast with the details of the psychiatric ward where your mother lies in bed, mentally ill because of abuse from her husband. The realistic images in the hospital seem like a palimpsest, and the detailed, well-informed images culled from your travels like wildly vibrant brush strokes on top. Is this how you see what you do?

**PP**: The images from my travels and from books come first. The excitement of the image comes first. I paint the family psychodrama on top of this base. For example, the poem 'Anaconda' originated from two books. One is a painting of the Sach'amama (a giant earth boa demon), by the Peruvian shaman artist Pablo Amaringo, in the book of his paintings *Ayahuasca Visions: The Religious Iconography of a Peruvian Shaman*. The details of my poem come from his vision of the giant boa and how she can mesmerise deer. She is so huge and slow-moving that trees grow on her! The other book that informed that poem is *Mother of God* by Paul Rosolie, an account of how he was almost eaten by a boa. I couldn't help but think of my mother and her depression, a condition I also suffered from.

**P McC**: Your work is full of metamorphoses, including in this latest collection:

> The brush paints backwards, removing the annatto dye
> that's protected me against your ghost,
> dressing me in red jaguar clothes.

How would you say these metamorphoses are particularly relevant?

**PP**: In this poem that you quote from, 'King Vultures', I found a way of writing about a particularly painful incident from when I was in my early twenties. My mother rang me and I stood in the hallway of the house where my bedsit phone was, while she told me how her psychiatrist told her she shouldn't have had children. I was depressed at the time, on meds myself, and she seemed oblivious to how her words made me feel. With a painful memory such as this it is very hard to write without being bitter, or angry with her, and I didn't want to make the poem about me. I wanted to be able to write her viewpoint without rancour, and with compassion. I still think what she did was wrong, but I'm glad I wrote the poem and felt her anguish at her ruined life.

When I was last in the Amazon I saw king vultures. I had before then only seen them in the Jardin des Plantes zoo. There is something about their creamy feathers and rainbow heads that is otherworldly, so I wanted to capture the freshness of their colours in my story. The story of my poem enacts a burial myth that my guide told me in the Peruvian Amazon – how shamen's corpses are left on a table under the buttress roots of a kapok tree for king vultures to eat, so they may be returned to the sky kingdom. I enact this ritual backwards, starting from my mother's death, to a time before my birth, giving her back her life without me. This metamorphosis of our lives into this ritual has helped me feel better about that phone call, because now I have the phone call, but I also have this version of it.

**P McC**: That's really interesting. The poem 'Musica Mundana' shows how you mix painting images with more profound themes such as your mother's death. Here, the persona is an artist, 'a painter of tropical flowers':

> ... But it was
> only when I added my mother's
> ashes that the painting seemed to come
> alive. I paced back and forth,
> rocked myself into the frame of mind
> to hear what paint has to say.

Would you say this is your poetic practice in general?

**PP**: Do you know Anselm Kiefer's recent flower paintings? They are extraordinary. He himself thinks they are too beautiful and mistrusts them. I saw them a few times, in Paris and London. The materials that are mixed in with the textures of the poem are his. I can't remember if he had ash, but I added that. My mother was not cremated, so it's fiction. I'd say at the crux of this poem is my method of writing, which is to try to get into a trance, to hear 'what paint has to say', what anything has to say that doesn't originate from my mouth, to see beyond my eyes.

**P McC**: Well said. I love the way you juggle with the real and surreal. Does this help you to 'be yourself and not yourself', as I think you said somewhere?

**PP**: I don't think there is anything surreal in my poems. All the images come from real life, things I've observed or read about. For example, the hummingbirds in one of the last poems in *Mama Amazonica*, in the poem

'The Hummingbird Whisperer', are laid out in my mother's body for the surgeon. Although she didn't have hummingbirds in her body, the image of them laid in rows comes from a photograph of hummingbirds in a suitcase with red lining. The red lining made me think of a body. So all I did was to juxtapose the two images. I admit that is a surreal technique, but also the basis for metaphor. The hummingbirds are in one of the ornithologist Augusto Ruschi's suitcases and in them he transported his birds in the hold of planes. I've used another version of this image in the first poem of my book *The Zoo Father*, a poem called 'The Strait-Jackets'. But this is actually a different suitcase to that one, and it was discovering this second photo with the red suitcase that led to this poem.

**P McC**: It appears that you always write in sequences. Do you plan these carefully before you start? For example can you tell us a bit about the book you are working on right now, and its ekphrastic slant?

**PP**: Ever since I heard about Cézanne and his Mont Sainte-Victoire, I have been drawn to work in sequences. I was a teenager then, and I remember being so impressed that he just kept returning to the same mountain to find new ways of painting it. I loved the obsession and single-mindedness of it. I thought: if I can be a hundredth as good and dedicated as that I'll be happy. So, yes, I do choose to work in motifs, until I've done a good job of painting my mountain.

**P McC**: I see your sequences as a series of painted panels. Do you?

**PP**: I see them more as galleries full of sculptures and installations, some videos too. But yes there are paintings and triptychs and diptychs and panels. Thank you for seeing them as panels. I don't trust myself as a painter so it's good to know they are for you. Colour is important to me, even when I made sculptures they were vividly coloured.

Thank you for your insightful questions, kind comments on my work, and interviewing me for *Agenda*.

**P McC**: Thank you, Pascale. It has been a pleasure.

# John F Deane

## Piano

Come stand awhile, here, at the outermost edge
of the world, the end and the beginning;
Ireland, Atlantic weathers, the cliff face sheened
with rain; sunlight glints off the schist diamonds,

a dusty dribble of stones splitters down into the sea.
Here the child knelt, on the window-seat, gazing out
at hard, inhibiting elements; on the upstairs landing,
in a cut-glass vase, Delft-blue and linen-white hydrangeas

stood in autumnal light; he could hear grandmother,
who dressed in black, sobbing behind her bedroom door.
The child was learning that there are stations of sadness
on the long journey, from *introibo* towards *amen*, because,

she told him, her years of dreams appeared to her, this late,
to roost like bats from branches of diseased elms. Stand now,
this precious moment, on the bridge at Achill Sound; watch
all the oceans of the world come teeming out of Blacksod Bay

to roar and crush through the gullet of the Sound;
at high tide there will come quiet, a still point, before the turn,
when all the oceans of the world come thrashing back
as if all cosmic being must depend upon it. His, then,

is the music of island, but sometimes there is another music,
in the great hall, that moves him; two dressed in black are seated,
edged, on black piano stools; there is a background
of indeterminate cloth, grey-black; the auditorium stilled,

a few small lights mark exit; two grand pianos are standing
poised, great wings spread; this will be Messiaen, *Visions
of Amen*, each piano challenging the other, each holding
to cliff and crossing, the beginning, and the end. Near

understanding, for the child, like walking barefoot over
bulwark stones, winds crying, while out at sea the whitest
gannets dive; on the strand, he can hear the calls
of oystercatchers, their black and white, their blood-red dagger-bills.

# Artist

Once, in the guest parlour of the monastery, two
grand pianos, winged and elegant, like seraphim;
on the pastel-coloured walls, stylized pictures:
Francis of Assisi and Anthony of Padua, lives
dedicated to their this-world other-world Christ.
Under shaky spotlights, the pianists; in the shadows
the guests, bemused, in feast day best, and smitten.
Mild applause. The pianists bow and settle. Two
fussed page-turners, the music of Messiaen furious
as thunder-burst, the harmony and counter-harmony
of creation, comet-falls of chords, chromatics, scales,
fingers and wrists of the priest-like bodies of the pianists
pre-occupied by sacrament. The guests all sitting, strained,
half-stifled coughs, a little self-conscious shuffling,
while above it all, in the night air, the monastery bell
waits silent, poised and ponderous in its louvred tower.

# The Trout

The river was beautiful, dark water running smoothly before the rocks,
silver-white and golden-ochre as it broke; below the rocks the pool, calm
as if in world-satisfaction, promise in its depths.

Father fishing; absorbed in the world.

When he had the trout up on the bank, the sorrow began within me;
that innocent lithe body, its gold-brown colouring, spots on its skin like
miniature haloes; eye wide, unmoving, lips hard, mouth gasping.

Father put his thumb inside, forced back the head and I heard bones
snapping. I almost wept; but this was my father fishing, who was spring
and flow for me; he was absorbed, then, in the world but I felt something
in creation's plan move towards disorder.

When the quintet stepped out onto the stage, I was sad, too; they were
elderly, white-haired, fumbly, the door banged back behind them as they
foostered towards the chairs, while I became aware of the hard bench
under me.

Three old gentlemen; one old woman, a younger one at the piano.

They sat, ordering themselves to a settling of instruments, bows and
strings, the piano stool, the tautness of the instruments like the stiffness of
the flesh.

I was dismayed. Schubert: *Die Forelle*. Then

they began. Within moments, it was father again, absorbed in the world;
there was an early summer breeze, the sun shone; stream-water sparkled,
fitting itself wholly into itself; earth a joy, azure the unattainable sky;
piano runs and playfulness, strings like lithe bodies in fluid mastery.

When I opened my eyes I saw them, the elders, flux and energy of their
bodies absorbed from one another, moving like reed-beds, like water-lilies
and it was love, it was the spirit breathing again through Genesis, as if the
seniors were extracting order and not imposing it; disparate they were,
shifting in their own breezes, yet shifting as one, their parts moving, the
whole refigured, segment and whole resolving.

I found myself, afterwards, exhausted, laid out on the green fields of the
world, hurt, and never so alive.

# John Freeman

## A Posy of Daisies in Sunday Meadow

Her name has given Peter Blake his cue,
painting her portrait, in his comprehensive
depiction of all the characters from
Llareggub in *Under Milk Wood:* Bessie
Bighead. He's given her a forehead
that bulges from the level of her glasses
up to the hairline so she looks like, I think,
Hugh MacDiarmid, Trotsky, or someone else –
which other man does she remind me of?
It's like that with a lot of these portraits,
and only when I've thought this for some time
do I learn that it was deliberate, unashamed:
the second narrator's Humphrey Bogart, changed –
slightly, different hair, added moustache and beard.
I'd thought it was Albert Camus, which shows
how like the two chain-smoking icons were.

The one that gave the game away for me,
so there could be no doubt, was Liz Taylor.
I'd not have guessed the face with woman's hair
was Terry Wogan's. Oh yes, James Joyce –
that was the other fellow Bessie Bighead
bears a likeness to, round glasses, that expanse
of brow under the slicked-back hair. Her picture
seems done with more elaborate care
than any other, layers like a palimpsest
of autumn leaves, transparent, one on one,
the living eye visible behind the lens
of the spectacles like Jimmy Joyce's.

The pathos of the dream kiss for one dead,
who had kissed her once when she wasn't looking,
and never kissed  her again though she, you know
the rest, but there's no punch line here, only
the poignancy of lifelong loneliness.

Was the painter right to depict her and him
as their lips close in for that second kiss
older, as she is now, dreaming of him,
and as he would have been if he had lived,
rather than as they would have surely been
in her dream, young, as they had both been once?
I doubted it, but now I'm sure he was.
The youthful selves are implied, implicated,
folded in, as the layers of sepia
fold on each other in this textured painting
which makes, as all the greatest art does,
something fulfilling out of unfulfilment.

# A Sky Reflected

If I hadn't had that pint in Kennedy's
on top of the half, and the red wine later,
I might not have lain awake till half past three,
and passed the time by fixing in my mind
what I'd gazed at before lunch, and again
afterwards, in the Hugh Lane Gallery,
the painting by Berthe Morisot of two
young women sitting in a boat, one watching
three ducks in the water and the other
looking straight at the beholder of the picture,
with such a vulnerable expression
she seems completely there in front of you,
affirming by her delicate openness
what it is to be properly alive,
responsive to the world and capable
of being hurt by it, by the same token
able to be moved to sympathy,
and to delight, and non-judgmental wonder.
What other painter could have caught that look?
There's something almost weak, almost unformed
about it, which makes it the more human.
No reproduction could convey its life,
I think, certainly not this postcard that I buy
anyway to remind me what it's lacking,
which is why if I could take away just one
of these great paintings – the Renoir umbrellas,
the Manet portrait or, my second candidate,
bearing in mind *unreproducability,*
the Pissarro figure in a landscape –
it would have to be this one. Every time
I strayed back in the actual gallery
to study it again, or do so now
with my mind's eye, having pictured it after
one too many Guinnesses hours later,
when it was still as good as there before me,
I get a different sense of what it is
that makes this composition so enchanting:
the girl's face on the left certainly, but then
the touches of red, so slight you could miss them,

the trees and sky reflected in the water,
the subtle broken greens, darker and lighter,
merging with blues as the attention travels,
where the lake reflects what must be white cloud.
I find one small and unobtrusive passage
of paleness tinged with blue that seems to bring
the sky down like a liberating presence,
a promise of freedom from all the constraints
on these corseted girls in bourgeois Paris,
a harmony of nature with conventions
which the pale questing face of the young girl
must after all be longing for a glimpse of,
and which in the vision of Morisot,
unlike in that of her brother-in-law,
collaborator, friend, and portraitist,
Edouard Manet, is not beyond attainment.

# Marie Papier (-Knight)

## Frieda After

*After Frieda Kahlo*

I have never painted
a tram since that fateful
day but blood,

arteries and my heart.
To keep myself straight
I drew the tram rails

and wrapped them
round my cage.
From that date

I painted myself as two.
Frieda before and
Frieda after.

We both married
the same man
who was unfaithful to us.

Our children grew in my brain,
a secret place
in-between the eyebrows.

I dressed them
before they were born
in ponchos and Oaxaca dress,

kept them in my head
where they'd be spared
and blossom on the canvas
of my mind.

# Peter Dale

## Dream On

Some sleep research concludes we never dream
of our own dead. But this is not the case.
Two decades dead yet still your voice and face
appear in dreams expounding our fond old theme
of poems, not verse – our lifelong two-man team,
touch-tones and quotes crisscrossing our shared space.
Fresh theories of yours my memory cannot place
in past discussions. New, as it would seem.

After a dream has had your latest say,
a settled calm pervades the living day.
It's strange, since dreams must be soliloquy.
Your voice must be some ventriloquial me.
Despite the doubtful memory of dream
I miss you. Which of us were one in our two-man team?

# Gerard Smyth

## Nolde

*(at the Nolde exhibition, National Gallery of Ireland)*

Walking through these rooms of Nolde's paintings
I notice that the sea is too silent,
a tree is waiting to be green again.

I feel nostalgia for the psychedelic era.
So many colours, so much razzle-dazzle:
nights of cabaret, a Friday afternoon on Calvary;

his isle of the blessed is idyllic, the people look happy.
There are poppies so scarlet they appear to suggest
a bloodletting. A man's face is distorted

by the five stages of grief or being unloved.
Hamburg is darker, boats on the Elbe
and boats in the harbour merge with the darkness.

Adam and Eve his sister wear only their vanity
and the couple wiggling their hips in a modern dance
must be shaking because there's a war in the distance.

# Shaun Traynor

## Sleeping at One Stafford Place, Huddersfield Rd.

(for Barry and Anne)

After the film*which was about young girls,
my sleep was fragrant with their movement,
how they combed their hair,
the flow of their bodies to the dresser;
In my own sleep they were a part of the territory of grace,
the music of Mahler, the writing on some pages
of the Alexandria Quartet;
so, they moved in a metamorphosis
from the ikons of my own dead youth
into the tormented unreality of waking dream.

In the morning, the rooks woke me with their bickering,
the thrushes and the blackbird tried to sing,
but whether from last night's over-use, or a sickness of pollen,
before the dew, their song came weary and unwashed...

only the wood pigeon let his deep-throated, breathing song
flute its way into my dream of bodies
and how with Barbara I might imitate
its rise, its fall.


*Picnic at Hanging Rock

# Ripponden

From Ripponden Bank, The Fleece, Barkisland.

Ripponden, my Canaletto village, where you hang,
I tell you there are times, when turning in a summer's day
I see you framed by haze and sky, and in your picture, fields
that lie beyond where I can turn my head.
Then, the picture breaks its frame,
for my poor words can never frame
the fields that lie beside a neighbour's fields
to form a circle of astonishment.

Ripponden, you are the centre of a summer's day.

How often have I stood on this high ridge
of your descending beauty,
and let my thoughts, like willow fronds
blow senseless by the hills;
I have made myself a part of Nature,
as intense, yet scared to move –
lest I disturb what God and farmers
have made beautiful.

# John O'Donoghue

## Restored

*after Sean Keating's painting* 'Goodbye, Father'

It's a scene from some lost classic
Of Irish cinema: the Aran Isles,
The flat strand after a great storm, shy smiles
As the Islandmen bid goodbye
Their portly, balding priest. The eye
Is taken by that suitcase on the shore:
Is his old black cassock
Folded neatly up inside, or

Is there perhaps poitin, a gift
They gave him as a souvenir? It's clear
What comes next. A close up of the priest's tear,
The skies darkening overhead.
Cut to the church, the wine, the bread,
The islanders' way of life restored.
Then the clouds as they lift,
And once more the great world ignored.

# Omar Sabbagh

## Loving Vincent

*For Faten*

The licks and daubs may flicker, savagely true,
And she has loved the show.

Scores of artists lend their ears, ears like canny doors,
And the whore at the source of the question

Finds a heap to listen to – bleeding there, red, and listening.
And if I were to cut my own, like some cheap, solicitous drone

Faced by an artist, sweatier, whose right was rightly wrong –
I'd see my song less deftly dreamy; for I love his knightly hue, pricked by
drunken stars.

In the cinema of our lives, in the desert of the same,
My love has more panache

In the name of her better name.  I cannot slash
Across a canvas with such visceral, filmic truth –

My licks, my daubs are meagre; they serve to serve the reign
Of the radical wand-strokes of a madly better man.

# David Cooke

## Three Rooms

*after Van Gogh*

i

## The Potato Eaters

There's a room elsewhere that's brighter
where food appears as if from nowhere
on plates so fine you can shine a light
through them: a feast for the eyes
before the palate succumbs to slick
lubricious juices. While here
they'll have no truck with a dish
that's pimped and primped.

For as long as the earth provides
they know they will always survive
on what is dug from claggy acres.
For as long as the fire endures
and the pot hangs on a hook
they will gather quietly around
their table. They peel back the skins.
The soft, white flesh blossoms.

ii

## On the Threshold of Eternity

This is the room where a man sits alone
on a simple chair, his body slumped
in a pose of bleak interrogation,
his tunnel vision to see each work
as a chart of flawed intentions,
his days locked in the bleared lens
of pointless despair, sensing too
beyond the flames of manic summers
that cold stars are turning,
tuned to a shrill monotonous note.


iii

## The Artist's Bedroom

Any room you like can be a refuge –
with three closed walls and a window
through which you glimpse the world.
One by one the walls collapse,
extending your view towards both east
and west, but then revealing everything
you thought you'd left behind. The low
ceiling lifts into a sky so distant
you forget sometimes it's there.

All that remains is a window
that you will slowly fill with bridges,
boats, faces, trees, some yellow, white
or purple flowers, the endless waves
of a cornfield above which a handful
of wind-tossed birds
seem to be holding their own.

# Staring at a Hoopoe

*ilare uccello calunniato*
  from Eugenio Montale's poem 'Upupa'

Caught in the moment,
there is no way of knowing
who might have blinked first –
the old man or his visitant,
the bright, crested
ambivalent bird. A few
scattered objects
implying a workspace,
the room is otherwise
unfocused beyond
the reciprocal stare
of two survivors.
The eyes of one are stoical,
but lit by a sense
that all is not determined.
The other's are steeled,
impenetrable – the maligned
harbinger of spring
or a bird whose piping
mnemonic call
is like a final summons.

# Sue Mackrell

## Vive La Parisienne

Impressionist men liked their women posed, and poised,
the bourgeois leisured lady, silk decorously arranged.
A wife or sister, lowered gaze focused
on seemly stitching, modest, deferent,
knowing her place.

And then there were the others,
'les cocottes de rue,' streetwalkers,
the flaneuse of Pigalle,
skilled in skirting the vice police,
assessing the quality of a silk scarf,
the provenance of a top hat, a finely cut frock coat,
the contents of a fine pigskin wallet.

These women are displayed
voluptuous in taffeta, flaunting  ample cleavage,
face painted, rouged, lipsticked,
displaying flesh for consumption
in suspenders and  laced boots.

'A woman who paints is ridiculous'.
wrote Renoir.

And yet, perhaps, in a squalid boudoir
or a red curtained Rococo bordello
where an old roué is spread sated on the bed,
a woman reaches in a bedside drawer
under the frilled chemises, striped stockings
and prophylactics, takes out a sketchbook
and draws, in gouache or charcoal,
smudging the edges with a wet finger,

The artist in repose.

# D V Cooke

## Opus Anglicanum

Arriving from the mundane
World, sitting around fire late,
Crackles laughter, doom and fate
With the kingdom to remain.

In firmament no portent
Nor word other than a casket
From whale's bone carved and inset
With magi and a rune lament.

Yet waking at the end of night,
Wordrich third millennium me
Filled with talk and poetry
Watches morning embroider light.

In the hills of poetry
Where the chaliced kingdoms come
To the new scriptorium
Wakes the sleeping memory.

Grown from one uncommon birth
Here the grave returns the womb
And the rightful bride in whom
Springs the laurel from the earth.

*Notes:*

*Opus Anglicanum* or *English work* refers to fine needlework of Medieval England done
for ecclesiastical or secular use on clothing, hangings or other textiles. *The Franks
Casket* held in *The British Museum* is a small nine inches by seven inches by five
inches whale's bone box from the eighth century. It is carved sometime pictorially
and with Anglo-Saxon runes and Latin inscriptions to various stories and myths from
among others: the *Trojan War* involving Achilles; *The Adoration of the Magi*; *the
fall of Jerusalem by the Romans*; *Romulus and Remus* and the founding of Rome
and therefore by implication to *Hengist and Horsa* and the founding of Anglo-Saxon
Britain. The Franks casket was once used in France in all its then unknown anonymity
as a commonplace sewing box until it was rediscovered and donated to the British

Museum in 1867 where it now resides in Room 41.

To unpack or uncompress the last stanza of the poem the casket is seen as a bride or womb or hollow box which once was used to contain needlework – (hence the *Opus Anglicanum – English work*, of the poem's title) but now its carved inscriptions and pictorial elements containing at least half-a-dozen mythical and historical stories have been culturally recognised and therefore it has as if arisen from the grave and has been awarded the laurel leaves.

# XXIX – Nicholas Hilliard 1600

Burnt black cherry stone best
For the art of miniature –
Burnt in a crucible, sealed
With a little salt her eyes are.
Or as white rose petals bruised
And ground to extract her colour,
So with a brush of squirrel hair
He paints her in miniature.

Carnation to colour her cheek.
Will you say her mind's oblique
But satisfies – his exquisite
Brush caught her mood before it
Fell and caught her so once more
She may blush into her grandeur.

Afterwards in autumn the blush
Had gone – only two cherry trees
Carved with her emblem, and these
Oval portraits now astonish.

*Note:*

See, *A Treatise Concerning the Arte of Limning* (1600) by Nicholas Hilliard (1547-1619), Court painter to Elizabeth I. Elizabethan small oval miniatures were limned or painted in water-colour on vellum normally by a fine squirrel-hair brush in open light with no shadow or chiaroscuro effects.

# Jessica Mookherjee & Simon Tje Jones

## Overboard

(Giorgio de Chirico *The Anxious Journey*)

One of our sailors is missing, the sky is stricken,
a torn timetable, as squall sets in.
The night before he leaves he wants to share
me, I'm on scullery duty and turn away.

There's an empty chair at check in, shorter queue
for meds. He's left
his compass, charts, three sheets to the wind,
I find dirt from his trousers, blind spot near wires,

a tunnel.

*He's just a boy full of wine-dark sea.* I hold the bench
so's not to fall in, tune
into silent periods before helicopters come.
They ask us for information and spin his room,

pile sandbags to stop a storm, ask questions
about his appearance and state of mind – nobody
speaks. I keep his place, his phone number, a towline.
One of our sailors is missing.

# Interview with Frieda Hughes

**P McC**: It is quite unusual to find an established poet who is also a fine visual artist, such as yourself, following in the tradition of William Blake and David Jones. Are you consciously influenced by either of these, or by anyone else? And have your paintings evolved since you studied at Central St. Martins College of Art?

**FH**: The desire to both paint *and* write wasn't influenced by any individual in particular, although images of Blake's artwork were sellotaped to the minute wall of the tiny toilet in the family home when I was a child. (I particularly remember 'The Ancient of Days', 'Satan Smiting Job with Sore Boils' and 'Illustration to Dante's Divine Comedy', together with a couple of Bosch colour prints.) I felt a need to do both because I had a sort of music in my head that dictated words, and a sort of itch in my hands to create things – pictures, dresses, bits of pottery, paper flowers. These two impingements on my consciousness developed into a compulsion to write and paint. Doing one and not the other was a little like eating to feed hunger but not drinking to quench a simultaneous thirst. Not doing either was like watching time pass by fruitlessly.

In the early years, I was highly conflicted by which of the two should get priority. In fact, in my early twenties I experimented by giving first one, then the other, a year of my devoted time. I fell short in both cases at three months. I recall being in the middle of a dinner with several friends and acquaintances at a local pub when, suddenly, I could no longer stand my self-inflicted ban on painting and had to go home to work immediately, leaving behind a perfectly good half-eaten steak.

But between 1984 and 1994 I stopped writing poetry (except for 'leakages', which I stuffed into the proverbial shoe-box-beneath-the-bed) because I feared comparisons to my parents. Instead, I concentrated on writing children's stories and painting.

My own logic dictated that I try to find ways for my painting and writing to work together, so I illustrated two of my children's books, although I hadn't intended to be an illustrator – I wanted to be a *painter*. I also used to draw a lot of animal – mainly cat – cartoons and was the cartoonist for *The West Australian Magazine* when I lived in Australia during the 1990s.

This was aided by the fact that I was, at the time of leaving college, a painter of detailed and decorative water colour, gouache and ink images. Even when I later moved into acrylics and oils I was still detailed; and I felt that my landscapes were static and surrealist: I painted the things I loved to paint in a way that I loved to look at them, which, however, did not describe how I *felt* about them.

Until, in 1994, when, while living in Wooroloo, Western Australia, I developed Chronic Fatigue (Myalgic Encephalomyelitis). As I lay, barely able to move some days, I wondered what I would like to do with the very short periods of time during the day that I could function at all, before I died (death always being the deadline). That was when I realised that I wanted to be free! I wanted to paint big, bold colourful paintings that expressed how I felt, instead of the carefully-constructed images that I currently laboured at. And I wanted to write poetry, not bottle it up because I might offend the sensibilities of complete strangers who would potentially damn me for being my parents' daughter.

And that is what I did. In the short periods of time I was awake during the worst of the M.E. which was seriously debilitating from February 1994 to summer 1997, I began painting big, bright oils on canvas, and writing poetry. The poetry was like a waterfall; having prevented myself from writing it for ten years, it was as if it had bottled up all that time and was just waiting to be released.

M.E. had forced me to examine the value of my days, which in turn determined the evolution of my art and writing; I stopped putting what I think of as 'societal' constraints on my work, and, as a result, felt that my work more accurately reflected the person I really was, and how I processed life. So, the evolution in my art, as well as my writing, has been considerable over the last thirty years.

**P McC**: You have said somewhere that you are addicted to both painting and writing poetry? Do you see the expression of both these forms in some way as cathartic or therapeutic, even subliminally? I remember a diary I read ages ago by R D Laing in which he describes how he rescued a woman from what was then presumed to be schizophrenia by staying with her day and night and getting her to express herself visually in paint – painting out her life – on the walls of the room she was confined to. She painted out her disturbance and came through it 'cured'.

**FH**: Writing and painting – certainly abstract painting – do have a therapeutic element to them particularly when the subject is myself, because working with my own reactions helps me process my experiences by facing them in an objective way. In writing particularly, I feel that setting down what has happened to me allows me to move on from it; an incident may have helped form me, influence me, and contribute to the making of the person I am, but the job of memory has been passed on to the page, so I no longer carry it. Also, by rendering something in poetry or paint there is a sense that one is 'heard'.

In painting my experiences I express my emotions, which helps to work them out of my system too.

One extremely important therapeutic aspect of the painting and writing is that, at the end of the process, I have created something where there was nothing before, which is incredibly satisfying. That it is a result of my verbal or visual description of simply *living*, is a joy because it demonstrates the 'recycling of self', where no experience, good or bad, is wasted.

**P McC**: That's a really interesting way of looking at it. This links to the 400 DAYS panel you exhibited in Chichester (wish I hadn't missed this) last summer as a kind of visual diary for each day. Interesting that you can paint a picture a day, but is it the same with a poem? Could you write a poem a day or do you have to wait for inspiration?

**FH**: I think it's entirely possible to write a poem a day, but the poems might not be very long, and it would devour time to do anything else. Which is what happened with my 400 DAYS abstract painting project. It was an idea that evolved from my wish to record daily emotions in response to happenings in colour and shape. I first did this over a period of five years, from 2000 to 2005, in a large project called '45', which was a series of poems and paintings based on the first forty-five years of my life. The resulting artwork was 45 panels measuring 4ft high and 225ft long, and a book of poetry published by Harper Collins in the US in 2006.

Having just finished an art exhibition in 2015, I was in the mood for another challenge, and so I started at the end of November (28th to be precise) 2015 to see if I could commit. By the time I got to December 31st 2015 I realised that the paintings looked extraordinary together, and created a sense of a whirlwind of energy; there felt to be something magical about them. So, then I just had to try and complete a calendar year – hence 400 days rather than 365.

My life came to revolve around the paintings; last thing at night, into the night, sometimes into the morning. On a couple of occasions, I had to miss a night because I was away (when my aunt died, for instance), and I'd do two paintings the next night, using my daily diary to base the missing painting on – they were, after all, a visualisation of my diary.

If I were writing a poem every day, would it be about my day? In which case it would double as a diary in the form of a poem. Or would it be about some other theme? Would it be any good without being driven by inspiration? Inspiration would be a big help – it is, after all, a driving force – but I think we can plod through something serviceable without. My paintings were very specifically about my days, and so became my visual diary. Now you have put it into my head, perhaps my diary could be put into a poetic form... after all, my poems describe my life, one way or another.

My new collection, '*Out of the Ashes*', which was published by Bloodaxe in May of this year, is a selection from my first four books with Bloodaxe, and spans ten years of writing, although the poems span my life.

**P McC**: Are the paintings – of your inner 'wasteland'? – expressing emotions that you can't or do not want to put into words? Do you ever attempt to 'translate' directly one of your own poems into paint? Your images are intensely original, sharp, tactile and visual. I am thinking of your poem, 'My Face' (from your collection, *Stonepicker*, Bloodaxe, 2001) – 'When I sleep, other people/ Wear my face'. There are lots of other examples that I can imagine being changed into paint, but sometimes more figuratively than abstract, maybe.

**FH**: A figurative response to a poem would be more of an illustration – although it does happen sometimes; there are a couple in *Alternative Values* simply because my emotional response to the poems in question demanded flowers. When the painted response is abstract then yes, it is all about how I feel in a visceral sense; I can rant in paint and it can look fantastic, but if I rant in the poem then I close the ears of my audience. In poetry, I want to present a situation, scenario or a case to the reader, and leave them free to have their own emotional reactions, but the painting is mine! If I want to be wanton, or angry or overjoyed in it, then I can, without deafening my audience. In *Alternative Values*, my book of paintings and poems, translating the poems directly into paint was exactly how the book came into being. The poems were the story and the paintings were my reaction to it.

You are correct that some poems lean more towards a figurative response – one day it might be interesting to paint one abstract and one figurative response, to each of a series of poems, in order to find out what happens...

**P McC**: I think that would be really interesting. It would be interesting, also, to know, hypothetically, if you stopped sharing your talents between visual art and poetry, and focused on only one, would that chosen art form then change? Do you think that, with the two forms, one compensates for the other, kind of?

**FH**: Interesting question! It rather takes me back to my answer to the first question: if I try to concentrate on only writing, or only painting, I become quietly, inwardly frustrated, and too introverted without access to expression in both mediums. It's as if the writing is for the ears and the painting is for the eyes, and neither discipline will accommodate both. When I'm working on a big project, then life sometimes dictates that too much time is being spent in one area, and then I become restless and irritable.

Does one compensate for the other? I don't think so. Would one discipline change if I did not do the other? I might be too frustrated to tell! But I imagine it would, as it would have so much more time allocated to it.

**P McC**: You said somewhere, and indeed you have already inferred here, that you examine your emotions through painting, and your thoughts through your poetry. Can you enlarge on this?

**FH**: In poems, my mind slices matters down to facts and happenings, imagery and the relationship between people; I aim to distil words in order to present a scene, or an idea, or an event in a direct way, so that the reader can engage and make the poem their own and relate to it how they choose. This is a process of analysing and directing my thoughts. But when I paint I want to fill the picture with the way I feel about that subject; I want to use colour and shape and to revel in the richness of the emotions (good or bad) that drive the image into being. There is a tremendous freedom in this. Then it is up to the viewer to decide what it means to them, and it is open to conjecture.

**P McC**: Yes, I like the way you kind of give away your poems and your paintings so that they can be interpreted differently and elastically by each different reader and viewer. Perhaps, though, are you, in your fine collection *Alternative Values: Poems and Paintings* (Bloodaxe, 2015), evolving to merge both your emotions and thoughts in your poems? Doing what you have called 'a little bit more of an unwrapping', making them 'a little bit more personal'?

**FH**: In *Alternative Values: Poems and Paintings* I wouldn't say that I'm merging my emotions and thoughts in the poems, because, as I have said, it is the paintings that describe my emotional reactions in order for the poems to remain clear, in the hope that the reader will apply their own emotional responses. The poems themselves have become increasingly personal, but in, I hope, a way that isn't muddied by emotion. I have written about my childhood, for instance, and, instead of embracing allegory, which is one of my favourite escapes if I want to get something out but not in an obvious way, I have been quite frank. It has taken me years to get to this stage.

My *Selected Poems*, published in May this year by Bloodaxe and called

63

'*Out of the Ashes*', comprises poems from my first four Bloodaxe collections, *Wooroloo, Stonepicker, Waxworks* and *The Book of Mirrors,* and it takes the reader on a journey through poems that used metaphor and allegory as a matter of course, particularly in *Waxworks*, where my father features as, for instance, 'Sisyphus', and I am represented by 'Madam Tussaud', to the later poems in *The Book of Mirrors*, which become increasingly direct in poems such as 'School Doctor', 'Preparing the Ground' and the first two poems about my brother, Nick, who committed suicide in 2009. So, over the years of writing poems there has been a definite evolution of self-exposure in, I hope, an entirely rational way. But the paintings will be where I continue to put the noisy expression of feelings.

**P McC**: That sounds very brave – the increasing self-exposure. But back to Blake and the way he incorporated his own handwriting into some of his art works. And now I am thinking of the front cover of the issue of *Agenda*, Past Histories, (Vol 43 No1) which contained one of a series of stained glass windows featuring animals and texts from your father's poems in the Yamada Room, Pembroke College Library, Cambridge, designed, engraved and etched on glass by Hans von Stockhausen.

I notice that, in some poems, you directly paste typed scripts of shortish poems over a painting. Would you not hand-write these, or wind them around shapes in your paintings somehow?

**FH**: Aah, I agonised about type on the white areas of the picture-pages in *Alternative Values*. In the end, I compromised – I left the spaces blank in the first photographs of the artwork for the printer, so that he could position the relevant poem in the book. But on the originals, I DID paint the poems by hand. In hindsight, I should have done that in the first place and photographed them for the book that way, but I was simply too concerned that people wouldn't be able to read my writing. After all, the words were written in oil, and it was a laborious job to try and get the paint thin enough to flow smoothly, often over an inconsistent surface. Whoever buys one of those paintings now gets my actual handwriting – the paintings have become artefacts.

**P McC**: In the final poems of the collection, in particular, you very bravely write quite directly about your childhood traumas: the depersonalisation you experienced in witnessing your parents' final row: 'So now I slipped between/ The folds in my head. My body/ Did things without me'. You even manage to cover your mother's last moments as she left you bread and milk 'before/She shut us in and Sellotaped the door'. 'Did I hear the silence when she ceased to breathe?' Then the strain when your grandmother seemed to wield a 'pickaxe' to get her grandchildren back to America, and the hugely moving final verse reminiscent of Homer,

I had already let myself slip through the gap
Between the floorboards of my consciousness
Until the fighting was over and the last body fallen.
But the fight just carried on and my father kept on falling,
My brother and I, tied to him
Like flailing arms.

That image there of your father and you two children stays in the mind like a haunting timeless sculpture.

**FH**: Those last three lines are, to me, probably three of the most powerfully evocative lines that I have ever written. I have such an image of my father falling through space, my brother and I not wishing to be parted from him, but then having to suffer whatever fate he suffered. When one falls, there is a sense of panic, of anticipation of pain, of fear of landing and breaking, of a wish to reel back time and undo whatever happened to cause the fall. As my father 'kept on falling,' all those feelings remain alive, unfinished, unrealised, anticipated and feared; the wind rushing past one's ears like a wail.

**P McC**: Terrible. In Memory Loss 3, you let the reader witness how you thought you had been adopted and were waiting for your real parents to arrive – perhaps a saving device for yourself? The memory loss which ensued and your gradual recovery left you with the sense that you were a 'changeling'. Although in these poems you are writing about particular events and details from your personal life, do you agree that, when the experience is so deeply lived as in your poems, the personal becomes universal: it could be anyone's trauma, whether imagined or similarly experienced?

**FH**: You mention recovery – in truth, I never recovered, but had to learn myself again. I became very watchful and felt estranged. I had to learn my name, and who everyone was, and what their relationships were to each other and me. It took a long time and I couldn't tell anyone for fear of upsetting the man I came to know as my father, whom I desperately wanted to protect.

Could the personal trauma become anyone's trauma? It depends how deeply a person identifies, I think. Sometimes another person's trauma echoes something of our own, despite fundamental differences, or someone writing of a trauma can convey it so successfully that the reader feels it to be familiar and 'recognises it', and/or is able to empathise with it.

**P McC**: In the fourth Memory Loss poem, 'Nesting', your disorientation is complete in 'the house of cards', what you then believed to be 'your borrowed home', with 'the boy who was meant to be my brother' and your father, 'surrogate or not'. The way you describe the houses you built for yourself with books and sheets 'to make a place my own' – 'A house inside the building/ He called home' is very graphic and could exist surely as a surrealist painting? Surrealism does seem to creep into your work?

**FH**: I did go through a surrealistic period for several years in the 1990s; some paintings contained people, others were based around rocks and trees. My description of the play-houses could indeed become a painting, although it is unlikely that I would be the painter as I steer clear of painting man-made objects. The play-houses were real; I was obsessed with making my 'own home' because I wanted somewhere that was mine, and where I felt I belonged.

**P McC**: That's such a killer. Interestingly in other poems, and even their titles, your language is perhaps more abstract than in your earlier collections – perhaps drawing the landscapes of your paintings into them? Yet the abstract paintings themselves take on all kinds of textures and shapes, tortuous arcs and tunnels but they are quite solid, and remind me of musical instruments, or even mechanical bits and pieces at times. Are they all symbolic to you? And although they are very much your own, is there a slight influence of Georges Braque here? Or even Calder when, for example, in the poem 'Purple Triangles', you talk about scraps of poems never used, asking to be freed:

> Their voices rise like coloured shapes
> Between these walls of books and paintings,
> Green squares, orange oval, and kites of purple triangles.

Here again, surely, you are visually painting with words that describe your actual paintings, so that your two art forms become one?

**FH**: This is where I have an advantage, being the artist and the poet in one! I can work the two together if the mood takes me, as in this case. There is no conscious influence from other artists, although sometimes I think the 1950s (colour, shapes, billboard-type impressions), snuck in somewhere and I can't imagine how. Mechanical elements such as motorbike engines and exhaust pipes, together with the organs of the human body, both requiring a 'connectedness of parts' in order to function, have always interested me, and might be subconscious contributors to my painted imagery. When I am painting what I feel about something, each shape and colour has enormous significance at the time it is applied, although I may later forget where it originated.

When my language includes elements that one would use to describe parts of an abstract painting, it is because I see everything I write about visually. Writing a poem (or a story) creates a film or a scene in my head, and that is what I try to describe.

Where the paintings are concerned, the shapes and colours are not exactly symbolic, but are produced when thinking about a certain happening in a poem, or a realisation, or an emotion – be it anger, happiness, joy or despair. They arrive on the canvas like notes from a piece of music from my head, as my mind plays the film clip of the poem I am recording in colour.

**P McC**: In your two-line aphorisms, backed by spiritual colours and textures of paint, as well as in some of your poems which are like little fables, with a lesson at the end, you come across almost as a guru, full of wisdom on how to live here on earth. Do think you have gleaned this because of the way you have, via your creativity, overcome the unfair share of traumas you have had in your life? And they have expanded you? Some of these paintings seem to depict an afterlife of sorts, for example, the painting with steps behind 'Life':

> Life is the forging of the spirit
> In the fire of experience.

Where do you stand on the hereafter?

**FH**: Thank you for the compliment! I mentioned before, I think of myself as a recycler-of-self; whatever we experience, see, hear, or learn, would be wasted if we didn't use it. With that in mind, I find myself looking at logic, and the consequences of action or inaction, in respect of events, drawing conclusions that educate me (I hope!) and inform me. Putting them through the distillation of poetry makes them, I think, more pronounced – more directed. I don't know if I can say they've helped me overcome anything but putting trauma into poems gives me more perspective and control, as I am effectively creating a new framework for them – my framework.

As for the afterlife, I have a feeling of urgency that I should 'get more done and fast' because my afterlife will be whatever I leave behind – although whatever I leave behind may find me irrelevant by then.

**P McC**: I hope not. You certainly come across as a spirited creator, and survivor against the odds. You have established very much your own identity as a poet and artist despite your immediate weighty literary heritage. You have never given in to 'falling in' which 'Would be to lose myself to loss/ And become pointless'. What has given you such strength to have such a positive approach, even after, as so movingly described in the poem 'Transition', your brother's sudden death by suicide, and your divorce, which changed you 'from being 'a wife and a sister to single in both senses/ That stripped my landscape of signposts, trees, definition and destinations', and capitulated you into a 'new wasteland'?

**FH**: To answer this, I have to say 'logic' is my last resort. When things fell apart – my brother's death, for instance, and my marriage ending – I had all the tumultuous feelings that anyone might experience; grief and loss can feel annihilating. And I felt annihilated. But if I apply logic... I believe that logic should be the back-up plan when we are emotionally incapable of making sensible decisions.

An example would be to tell you that I didn't want to get out of bed until the pain of loss had passed; I wanted to hide away like a withering slug under a chilly rock, and of course, I felt I wouldn't *ever* recover. But when I looked at myself logically, knowing that all things must pass (good as well as bad), and that if I could just accept the emotional pain (since, for me at least, denying it is futile and only prevents any positive change) and let it flow over me like the sea, then eventually things *must* change because that is their nature. Death of those close to me is not something that I think I should 'get over', exactly, so much as assimilate and adapt to, in order to 'grow beyond' the loss; the loss then becomes part of the weathering that forms me. (This makes me sound a bit like a rock formation!)

Moving on from that initial thought, I then have to accept that if I am going to survive the period of weathering this sea of pain, I need to make sure that my body functions – so eating properly is a must, and sleeping is more important than I can say. And I have to be strong physically, because the alternative is that I'll one day emerge from pain as a jelly-like blob, so I force myself to the gym three times a week. (Emerging from one pain as a blob would only create another kind of pain!)

To get through each session I put myself in front of a piece of equipment, look at the clock and think 'I can sit here and do nothing for ten minutes, or I can use the equipment, and in ten minutes it will be over'. Which would be the logical choice? I think of my body as a container that I would like to be in decent enough shape for happiness to later find root; it is my small effort in being prepared for a more positive outlook.

I ask myself 'is it logical that I make myself useless?' Or 'is it logical that I sit and cry, when I could pick up a paintbrush – and still cry?' I don't regard happiness as a 'right' but as a by-product of other efforts. To move forward requires constant effort, but every achievement, no matter how small (it could be as mundane as cleaning out a litter-tray) spurs me on.

**P McC**: You obviously love your home in Wales with your owls and the rest of your menagerie. Are your animals your muses? And do you find inspiration from the Welsh landscape, particularly for your paintings?

**FH**: My animals and my home are my preoccupation! They fill my need to care for things, and because I work at home, my surroundings are important. My owls are also sometimes my models – but not exactly my muses. The small owls live in the house, with a snowy owl that can't fly. I hand-reared two of the big Eurasian eagle owls when they were given to me as eggs together with their rather scratchy parents; they come in to the kitchen every evening to 'play around' for a couple of hours. It is a ritual, and sometimes they're waiting at the door almost stamping their feet to come in.

In respect of landscapes, I have only ever really loved two places in my life, and with a passion; the hamlet where I lived in Western Australia in the 1990s, called Wooroloo, which is also the title of my first poetry collection, many of the poems of which are included in *Out of the Ashes*, published in May, and mid-Wales, where I live now. Their landscapes make me want to paint them for as many years as I have left.

**P McC**: Let's hope you have many years, Frieda! Let us finish by thinking again of David Jones, the Welsh bard, who saw all the arts as one: 'Poetry, painting, carving are only as different as oil paint and watercolour'.Would you agree?

**FH**: I do think of the arts as one, in the sense that in each, we make shapes, or images, or sounds, or tell stories and conjure ideas out of raw materials to describe something we have seen, experienced, thought, or something within us. To me, art is that use of raw materials in a descriptive way, a way that distils or crystallises an idea to form an end product that can be seen, read, heard or touched by others, where before there was nothing.

Then we have accomplished something.

**P McC**: Well, thank you very much indeed for such an inspiring, interesting and bravely honest interview.

# Frieda Hughes

## Blue Hippo

Open mouthed
My brother's blue hippo calls into the air
For his father.

Fingers through which blood pulsed, flexing muscle and sinew
That are now ash, had stroked its clay flanks into
The powerful rounds that shine mutely in blue beneath
My landing light, solidly planted on four hippo posts
To support a head as big as its torso.

The mind that made it
Had walked the banks of Lake Victoria in Africa,
Skirted Alaskan rivers, and climbed Irish hills.  Devon moorland
Had claimed the pattern of those feet, so that
Somewhere in that wilderness my brother's footsteps
Still litter the undisturbed earth
Where they have not yet been trodden over.

There were no children when he left, just
Four kilns, banks of powdered pigment,
Experimental colouring mixes
In maddeningly narrow degrees,
And one large blue hippo.

# Abegail Morley

## *Baño* Británico

*After Fernando Vicente*

She fetched the ocean from two continents away,
allowed the moon on its tide to wink across
her skin, splinter its way over the knuckle of each rib,
pool in cinematic slow-motion
in the tip of her belly.
Now, in the dark, she sifts through sand,
abandoned shells, watches for dabberlocks
with huge dark eyes.

She waits for the cool brush of water
to wash its final breath from the lips
of its almost forgotten mouth,
shudder its way down
her herring-thin spine to a hip bone
that juts like a spit
bickering with the sea.
She waits like this in a sprawl
of bed sheets, until the uneasy light
from the landing stalls,
the stub of its flame, blunt.

# Shell

'Measures of Deep' *by Valerie Condor*

When she raises it, it's weightless as a butterfly's wing,
a wren's egg that's lost its fledgling. She carries it in anyway,

aloft (for drama) and the bare floor beneath her feet creaks
in sympathy as if she pulls a knot from each plank's tight

hemming stitch. I shake it out of her hand without caution,
death no longer makes me shudder, I've washed

both the sun and moon away in the bathroom sink.
Once you've done that, little else matters. So I let her clatter

on the stairs like erratic shingle settling on the shore,
know sometime soon we'll sit and talk it through. I watch

as she self-seeds herself in mirrors up the stairs.
My uncremated twin, just a finger-pull away, is crying now.

I know he's curling into a tiny comb, pulling in his limbs,
his ears – just waiting to disappear in wax and pollen.

# Sally Festing

## The Question of Uncle Ben's Balance

*(from a sequence)*

Gentle, sweet, good-mannered Ben.
You read the Bible end to end.

For a brief equilibrium,
you moved to the big house.

How you loved the grapes that draped
the conservatory, the Beauties of Bath

you pruned. The garden of rocks
you hauled up stone by stone.

The carvings you chiselled
in hardest wood.

Katherine was a gift given to you
and your heart drowned in her –

As hedgesparrows made love
you kept toeing the tightrope.

*


Stuck in some accident of time,
you hallucinated.
Your face changed shape (the vertigo).
You wore a mask.
But your body's pain was paper-thin
and disposable
compared with that of your mind.

A shudder under your pale
bleached skull.
A shift in the hollow of your head.
Your heart's
stone
weighed you down. The rope
stretched
and sagged, dropping you into
darkness.

## What Survives is Gold

Four pm., and you've gone.
A fussing sun. The garden's bursting.
That heron has gobbled the last flash
from the pond. The fledgling in the rambler

is set to fly.
              Dithery, I bake a cake,
sifting into your skyscraper office,
your bravesmile, sucked fingers,
as you press on, wait

for the telephone. Waiting is worse
than disappointment, and your pain
is also mine.
                        Remember,

still at school you asked five friends
or was it six, to play? One by one they all
cried off, except for Milly. She turned up
true as a wet stone's shine.

Next time you come, you'll flop your mane.
Arm in arm, we'll taste the garden.
You'll flick your hand among the lilies,
laugh, *Let's buy more goldfish*.

# W S Milne

## Apocalypse

*'The Pricke of Conscience'*
   Stained-glass window, All Saints, North Street, York

near the last of days
the sea shall rise
high as Everest
the second day
to fall again
to the abyss
the day after this
level as a meadow
it will be
but on the day after that
the fish will go crazy
poisoned to the last
roaring their misery
the fifth day dawns
and the sea catches fire
burning till sundown
through the night and the next day
on grass and tree
mildew falls
rotting every apple
the morning after
every spire topples
every castle
till the eighth day breaks
and the rocks melt with the sun
every stone consumed by fire
and on the ninth
the people run
shelter in caves
the worst quake since time began
stare on the tenth
as the sky turns red
and the earth's stripped plain

mad with fear
on the eleventh
from caves they come
praying
till the stars all fall
the planets hurtle
as the twelfth day dawns
and on the thirteenth
the dead rise
shaking their bones
on the fourteenth
all who are living then shall die
to rise again
to joy or pain
on the last day of all
the world dies
in cinders and flame

# Myra Schneider

## In the Moment

After 'Tatekawa in Honju' *by Hokusai*

Relishing the taste of sweetness in this small
chill hour I turn to the January scene
on the wall calendar. The dark month

instils such a sense of doom but in the print
light is cramming a yard. How it revels
in the azure and white of the Tatekawa river –

not a hint of gloom here. Series of poles rise
like pinnacles above the violet-blue hills
and on the ground timber lies pell-mell,

juts over the water and in packs is piled high.
A labourer, back bent, is perched on one
that towers above docile village roofs.

The blocks of wood he's just hurled are flying
through the air towards his mate below.
I can feel the thrust of the thrower's arms,

the receiver positioning himself to catch –
it's a skilled dance, I'm hooked by the two men.
Yet in this moment I'm in my night-time kitchen

eating a banana and far from the yard in Japan,
its agile workers and timber intruding on sky –
the moment an artist stopped, began to draw.

# Tiger

After Henri Rousseau

This is not the tiger which burns bright,
not the silent forest of the night.
The wind rampaging in this tropical forest

is roaring with manic delight as it clenches
hapless trees, heaves trunks,
snaps twigs, twists branches.

Lightning strikes, no majesty here.
The tiger snarls, you can smell its fear
as a heavy branch cracks, falls,

ignites and becomes a vermilion tail
which will spread greedy fire. The sky
blackens. Crouched in the leafery

you watch the beast moving, body
low, fangs bared but not to spring
on prey. Look at its alarmed eyes,

it can't see how to attack noise,
unsteady trunks or maddened leaves.
Suddenly you know this jungle craziness

isn't without but rooted deep within,
know the fear under your corset of bones,
is the tiger, the shocking gleam in its stare.

# John Gladwell

## Leaving Departure

From the texture of your kiss to your skin
To the weight of your hand resting carefully against mine
Against the pull of the tide    of sunlight on water
Of foam at this water's edge   where I now stand
Looking out towards the windfarm and a sea-fret moving
A dream of frost   of the wind biting   of your lips bleeding
Leaving departure   leaving a strange bitter taste on my tongue
Seaweed and bladder-wrack and a drop of rain now freezing
Against your smile   against the edge of each tear as it falls

# Gary Allen

## The monster

When I was a child
and full of a child's anxieties
my father would let me stay up late
to watch the Frankenstein movie
though as I grew older, I thought it more from spite
than indulgence

the almost Orson Welles backdrops
the Eastern crosses, the skeletal windmill
the old woman pulling the monster out of the open grave
the closed taverns, the hunchback, the blind man
like tarot cards laid out to warn of disaster

and then, when I was half way up the stairs
he would put the light out
and shout, Here's Frankie
leaving me not sure whether to go on or turn back

caught in that fear of the unseen, the unknown
like whether my father would come back from working on the border
or my mother die in flames at the back of a firebombed shop
or playing games coming home from school
as to which car would be the one to explode.

# Judith Wilkinson

## The Whole Mosaic – A Day In The Atacama Desert

*'Why are there archaeologists and astronomers in one place? Because in the
Atacama the past is more accessible than elsewhere'*
                    Patricio Guzmán, *Nostalgia for the Light* (film documentary)

At the observatory an astronomer
scans the sky for treasure:
clusters of stars, nebulas, planets,
comets like those that watered the earth,
or the death throes of a supernova,
hatching our atoms.
Here the Chilean sky is so translucent
that he can almost finger the stars, pull them down
to eye-height, unravel the energy prizing them apart,
as if the story, from start to finish,
was his birthright.

In this salt-steeped land an archaeologist
studies strata of sand and rock
underpinned by meteorites
distorting the direction of his compass.
Tenacity got him this far, all the way to
rock face carved by pre-Columbian shepherds,
whose mummified remains he gathers up,
tracing each part to its origin.
He finds a petrified lake, with fish frozen in time,
and an ancient trade route from the high plains to the sea,
where caravans of llamas once found their way.

Near the ruins of a concentration camp, women
sift through the desert, decade after decade,
in search of loved ones.
Stumbling on Pinochet's mass graves,
they piece together what they find:
splinters that are worlds apart, bleached by the calcinating sun.
'I found a piece of my brother there
and spent a morning with his foot,
stroking it, though it smelled of decay,
hoping to find the whole mosaic
that was my brother'.

# Carolyn Trant

## Artists' Books

**The Untenanted Room**: James Simpson, Poems
Carolyn Trant, artist
(Parvenu Press March 2018)

James' poems were originally published by *Agenda Special Editions* in 2011 with small monochrome woodcut images I designed specially for that format. This new version is very different in size and scale – more like *Gawain*, my very first large woodcut Artists Book made in 1997 – with some coloured images spreading across two pages. Trying to break down barriers of 'text' and 'illustration' – sometimes the images take up the story and run with it, sometimes the poems stand alone. The texts are hand-cut in wood, reinforcing, in this digital age of easy reproduction, that these words are worth spending time with.

We are coming up to several centenary anniversaries – Jessie Weston's *From Ritual to Romance* published 1920, which in turn influenced Eliot's *The Waste Land* 1922 (see the last issue of *Agenda*), and the novels based on the Grail Stories of neglected modernist Mary Butts – *Ashe of Rings* first published 1925. The old stories retain resonances from past times and set up new ones. Designed for re-telling, they are still relevant in fractured times.

James' text flickers between a variety of current events and concerns, using a scaffold of the medieval story of *Perceval,* The Holy Fool. I am trying to mirror the metaphors of the writing with the way I print. Shreds of allusions and references in the imagery activate collective memory and things seen and half remembered, visual metaphors forced into new composite juxtapositions. Here for *Agenda* we have chosen the more conventional spreads showing text and image – especially as the images will not be in colour.

'Current events and concerns' are the perennial ones – man's inhumanity to man and the continual degradation of the planet, a Waste Land indeed. The first image is of an unspecified bombed building, in the Middle East maybe; later bodies hang like meat from the trees, the woodcuts try to flicker like TV screens, dead birds are strung up, trees look blasted. But art ultimately makes things look aesthetic, cosy. I try to be raw but pages inevitably become cooked – our conscience and consciousness makes things acceptable so that we can carry on. I hope this is an angry book all the same. I wanted it to be quite rough and immediate, not pretty at all; and James is in agreement – we pass ideas back and forth between us all the time.

The books combine being painted and printed. I always print like a painter anyway – so the blocks are just another way of getting colour and image onto the paper – and each book, from a very small edition of seven, is slightly different, each unique, bound within wooden boards. Woodblock printing with hand-painting is an old tradition but here it looks contemporary. The leather spine revealing the boards laced on looks conventional at first sight but is made using second-hand leather clothes with their seams and stitching retained: 'up-cycling' a bookbinder told me, approvingly I think. The wooden covers are papered with textured wallpaper, roughly painted so that they simultaneously reference – perhaps net curtains, rain on glass, a peeling wall, light glimpsed through forest trees? – a world in limbo, unresolved and uncertain.

James Simpson is a Jerwood/Arvon writing fellow and was a prizewinner in the Thomas Hardy Society's James Gibson Memorial Poetry Competition. His poetry has been published in *Agenda*, *The London Magazine*, *Resurgence* and The Hardy Society Journal and has been anthologised in *Our Common Ground* (Silverdart Publishing). Readings include appearances at the Cheltenham Literature Festival, the North Cornwall Book Festival and the Exeter Poetry Festival. He has collaborated with the artist and printmaker Carolyn Trant on the artist's books, *Hunting the Wren*, *The Rhyme of the Reddleman's Daughter* and *Some Light Remains* (all Parvenu Press); editions of these now reside in private and public collections nationally and internationally; including the British Library (Modern British Special Collections), Yale University Library, Louisiana State University (LSU Libraries) and the University of Georgia (Main Library). *The Untenanted Room*, was published by Agenda Editions in 2011 with woodcuts by Carolyn Trant.

Samples from the book follow.

A thin place in a thin time;
the blood bracked shuddering
in all the glass night;
and we the taut marchers and frost merriers

clasped onto earth's compass
and the crest capped haunches;
singing nights' crystal
and the ward welled blessing.

Through night's branches gleaming
like starlings over hillsides
and the breast papped chalk-lands,
lighted like candles and guttering torches.

Ours is the singing of the antlers blazing,
ours is the claim of the boar tusk whittling,
freeing the midden of the oak tree island,
singing the night and the unforgetting.

Sift, sift my love
and take a snatch of honey
in your mouth.

The bees come to suckle you
husk upon little husk,
it is a mean breath they offer.

Shh, there are no flowers
bless the rain on summer bowers,
let me tear each leaf in three

to twine around my fingers
bind and unbind to find an end,
this the art to which I am given.

Lullay, lullay, my little liking,
let me cradle you in this shroud
like a leveret in his coffin.

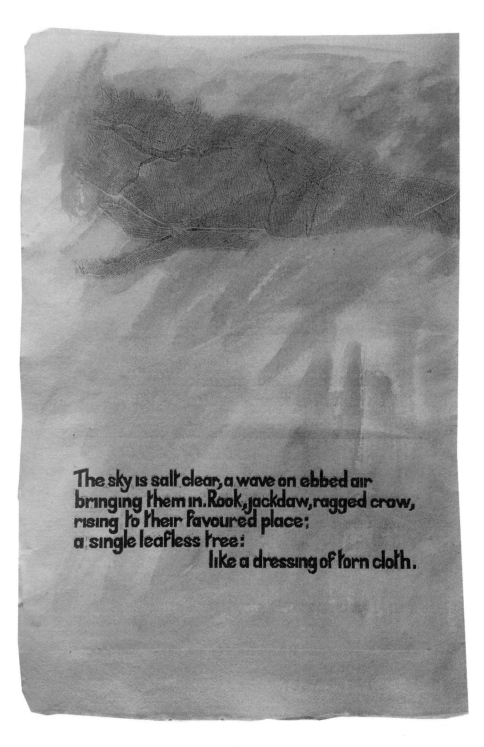

The sky is salt clear, a wave on ebbed air
bringing them in. Rook, jackdaw, ragged crow,
rising to their favoured place;
a single leafless tree:
                    like a dressing of torn cloth.

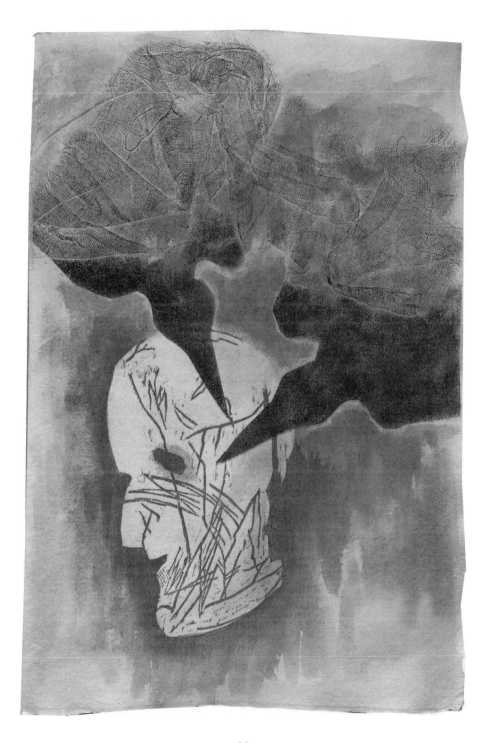

The cawing stops.
Only wind in the trees.

Before him a woman lies wounded;
her naked body curled like a shell.
He is on his knees.
What has he done?

He has no idea.

I have marked the dead seasons
one by one:
heard the footfalls fall again,
fall in a night

so dark, that hills and sky
were one in sound
and still: but for the unusual air
twisting in the beech leaves.

What mysteries are these?
this mouthpiece uttering,
the moon's limed walls.
Honest tongue,

there is nothing to be said:
this is the time of candle care
when frost lays
bitter the partial ground:

the lark has spun
the world on its axis;
and the blood
we have shed is mutual.

# Kim Moore

## Returning the Gaze: Poetry and Everyday Sexism

In *Ways of Seeing*, published in 1972, John Berger wrote, 'We only see what we look at. To look is an act of choice.' What do we choose to look at in poetry? What do we choose not to look at? Recent social media campaigns such as #MeToo, #TimesUp and the Everyday Sexism movement have shown that focusing on individual experiences of sexism can be a powerful tool in naming and raising awareness of gender inequality and abuse. However, it is difficult, if not impossible, to find poets tackling the topic of sexism in a sustained way, over the course of a whole collection. This is despite sexism being something that most, if not all women, experience.

In 2016 I began a creative-critical PhD to explore experiences of everyday sexism through poetic practice. Sexism is a structure in society, with the everyday experiences of it inextricably linked with more serious sexual assault and abuse. In *Living A Feminist Life* Sarah Ahmed writes, 'We need structure to give evidence of structure. To catalog instances of violence is to create a feminist catalog... we show what we know: that this or that incident is not isolated but part of a series of events: a series as a structure'.

The choice to 'look' at experiences of sexism has resulted in poetry which places men and masculinity in the centre of a poetic frame. We have so many words for different ways of looking – gaze, watch, see, glance, peruse, stare, observe, study, examine, regard, scan, gawk, glare, scrutinize, consider, peek, peep, ogle and survey. The word 'look' seems to be full of movement and implies not just the act of looking, but the act of looking away. To 'gaze' according to the Oxford English Dictionary, is to 'look steadily and intently, especially in admiration, surprise or thought.'

The opposing narratives around the 'male gaze' and the 'female gaze' have been particularly important to my research. In 1975, Laura Mulvey published her ground-breaking essay 'Visual Pleasure and Narrative Cinema'. She examined the male gaze in relation to film theory, pointing out that on screen, women are represented as objects of male pleasure and subjected to a 'controlling and curious gaze.' The male gaze portrays women in the way that men want them to behave.

At the 2016 Toronto International Film Festival, Jill Soloway (producer of hit TV shows like 'Transparent' and 'I Love Dick') called for the activation of the female gaze, describing it as a 'socio-political justice-demanding way of seeing'. She argued that the female gaze was a way of 'feeling-seeing', of 'privileging the body and emotion' and lastly, a way of 'returning the gaze, not just in the act of looking back, but to say "I see you seeing me"'. It is this last part of her definition of what it means to activate the female gaze that I think is particularly relevant to poetry.

Poetry about sexism says 'I see you seeing me'. It privileges the 'body and emotion'. It is a way of 'feeling-seeing'. Through writing poetry about sexism, I've discovered that sexism is a slippery and fluid term. It resists boundaries and definitions to encompass harassment, oppression, abuse and assault. Looking at sexism often causes it to change shape, to shift, to move. The label of sexism often becomes a coping mechanism in itself, used to shrink a traumatic or disturbing experience into something more manageable, something almost trivial.

Poetry steps into this space and forces us to look closer, look harder, at what we may have told ourselves was nothing. Often stories of sexism, particularly everyday sexism, have an absence at their centre. This idea of 'nothing' is something I return to again and again in my creative and critical work. The word 'nothing' becomes an effective protection, a wall to stop the mind imagining not only what could have happened, but also what the world might look like if these things didn't keep happening.

One of the reasons that lyric poetry is a suitable form to use to examine these experiences is because of its form. Jonathan Culler writes about 'the lyric convention of significance' – an unspoken agreement between the reader and the writer that whatever has been set down as a poem is important or elevated. Culler writes, 'The convention that whatever is written will prove to be important is particularly powerful, and crucial to the functioning of many modern lyrics especially'. The act of placing the white space of a lyric poem around experiences of sexism elevates their importance, making it harder to minimise or discount. Sara Ahmed writes, 'The past is magnified when it is no longer shrunk. We make things bigger by refusing to make them smaller'.

## All The Men I Never Married No.30

Imagine you're me, fifteen, the summer of '95,
and you're following your sister onto the log flume,
where you'll sit between the legs of a stranger.
At the bottom of the drop when you've screamed
and been splashed by the water, when you're about
to stand up, clamber out, the man behind
reaches forward, and with the back of his knuckle
brushes a drop of water from your thigh.

To be touched like that, for the first time.
And you are not innocent, you're fifteen,
something in you likes that you were chosen,
it feels like power, though you were only
the one who was touched, who was acted upon.
To realise that someone can touch you
without asking, without speaking, without knowing
your name. Without anybody seeing.

You pretend that nothing has happened,
you turn it to nothing, you learn that nothing
is necessary armour you must carry with you,
it was nothing, you must have imagined it.
To be touched – and your parents waiting at the exit
and smiling as you come out of the dark
and the moment being hardly worth telling.
What am I saying? You're fifteen and he is a man.

Imagine being him on that rare day of summer,
the bulge of car keys makes it difficult to sit
so he gives them to a bored attendant
who chucks them in a box marked PROPERTY.
A girl balanced in the boat with hair to her waist
and he's close enough to smell the cream
lifting in waves from her skin, her legs stretched out,
and why should he tell himself no, hold himself back?

He reaches forward, brushes your thigh with a knuckle
then gets up to go, rocking the boat as he leaves.
You don't remember his face or his clothes,
just the drop of water, perfectly formed on your thigh,
before it's lifted up and away by his finger.
You remember this lesson your whole life,
that sliver/shiver of time, that moment in the sun.
What am I saying? Nothing. Nothing happened.

In his book *Theory of the Lyric,* Jonathan Culler points out that it is rare for lyric poems to directly address the audience or reader, and that the usual mode for lyric poetry is what he calls the 'triangulated address', where the speaker of the poem addresses the audience indirectly by use of an apostrophe, addressing an unseen lover, or God, an object, animal or a more general, unspecified audience.

In practical terms, it's easy to see why. If an audience is addressed, the implication is that a response is needed, and a poem needs silence to be heard. Addressing an audience directly is a risky strategy, and to address a reader through a text, or an audience whilst performing a poem, the poet has to negotiate the shifting sands of the pronoun 'you' which can mean both the self, and/or the 'you' who is reading this poem, or listening to these words. In 'All The Men I Never Married' I wanted the 'you' to be a clear and direct address, so used the word 'Imagine' as the first word in the poem, a specific instruction to the reader or audience. I return again to Jill Soloway who said that the female gaze is a 'conscious effort to create empathy as a political tool' and a way of 'changing the way the world feels for women when they move their bodies through the world'.

Claudia Rankine referred to her book *Citizen: An American Lyric* as a 'documentary text', explaining that she began to gather 'small private experiences of racism from her own life and from friends'. *Citizen* is radical in its use of form and intertextuality, incorporating images and found text, and using this commitment to genre-bending to confront experiences of racism and sexism. She focuses in particular on the systemic nature of these discourses and the importance of making a connection between events. As Sarah Ahmed points out 'To mark a connection is thus to restore what has been lost (where loss should be understood as an active process); it is to generate a different picture'.

Throughout the text, Rankine also uses the pronoun 'you'. The reviewer Dave Coates pointed out in his blog review of *Citizen* that 'its recurring use of the pronoun "you" is partly an attempt to circumvent whatever defence mechanisms we might have against the idea we might be complicit in racial oppression'.

Poetry as documentation, as feminist work. Poetry as testimony. Sarah Ahmed writes, 'When you become a feminist, you find out very quickly what you aim to bring to an end some do not recognise as existing'. Poetry as social engagement. Poetry as epideixis – public discourse about meaning and value. John Berger writes, 'We never look at just one thing; we are always looking at the relation between things and ourselves'. Poetry as a way of looking. Poetry as micro-observation. Poetry as experiential, not personal.

In her 2005 book *Consorting with Angels: Essays on Modern Women Poets*, Deryn Rees-Jones argued, 'The dynamic set-up between autobiography and experience, as mediated into an aesthetic, and the value of experience in relation to women's poetry, becomes a crucial issue, specifically within feminist debates concerning the value of the personal to the political'.

In a world where a model can receive death threats for posing with body hair, it's clear that realistic portrayals of women's experience are needed.

# All The Men I Never Married No.10

Although we've only just met, he's already telling me
that no, my suitcase isn't heavy at all, as he lifts it
with one hand into the boot.

He's not even reached the end of the road
and he's already telling me I have a crazy soul,
that he can tell how crazy I am.

He asks me do I know what he means and I smile
and pretend that I don't. He says all the women
he knows who are artists or poets or musicians are crazy.

Crazy, crazy, crazy he says and I wish I'd told him
I was an accountant instead, but on he goes,
taking his eyes off the road

to tell me all women who are artists are crazy in bed,
do I know what he means, they want to try
crazy things in the bedroom.

If he stops the car I could open the door and run,
or pull out my phone and pretend someone is calling,
or ask him politely what's wrong,

or laugh at the next thing he says or maybe the voice
in my head will whisper that I've led him on,
that I was asking for it.

I remember a train journey, everyone crammed in
and a stranger's penis pressed against my leg,
convincing myself

I was imagining it, or he couldn't help it,
where else in the place could he put it?
When we pull up at the airport

my arm flings open the door before I give it permission,
my left leg finds the pavement before I can think.
Still I turn back to give him a tip,

and he's laughing, saying *relax, just relax,* and I know
that he knows I'm afraid, that I've been afraid all my life,
but it's not this that makes me ashamed.

On numerous occasions after performing this poem, men have come to
me afterwards and told me that this poem in particular makes them feel
'guilty for being a man'. Friends and strangers have both used this word
guilt. Once it happened twice in the same week.

I am trying to understand my own feelings of anger, when this happens,
which isn't quite like anger, not quite impatience, not quite disappointment.
I'm trying to understand their guilt. But I keep coming back to Audre Lorde,
who said, 'I cannot hide my anger to spare your guilt, nor hurt feelings, nor
answering anger, for to do so insults and trivialises all our efforts. Guilt
is not a response to anger, it is a response to one's own actions or lack of
action. If it leads to change then it can be useful, since it is then no longer
guilt but the beginning of knowledge.'

When men admit feelings of guilt for behaviour that they have not carried
out, the conversation changes from being about an experience of sexism,
to being about their feelings, about their story, their narrative. Often I
placate these men, who are often friends, or colleagues, or strangers. 'Of
course I'm not writing about you, about men like you. Of course, of course,
of course'. Or I ask them why, and they tell me their story, which might
involve their own experience of abuse by a man, but rarely touches on their
own complicity in sexism.

My friend says that I should answer not with reassurances (Of course I'm
not writing about you) but with a question 'That's interesting – what are you
going to do about it?' An admittance of guilt swings the poetic camera, the
poetic frame back onto the person who noticed that something was wrong.
Sarah Ahmed writes, 'You can cause unhappiness by noticing something'.
Is it possible to also cause guilt by noticing something?

## All the Men I Never Married No.33

when I tell them about my body
      and all the things it knows
they tell me about their guilt

they flourish their guilt
      like a matador fighting a bull
in a city where people love blood

or they wave their guilt at me
        as if it is a flag of a newly formed country
and they are proud to be citizens

sometimes they hold their guilt in their right hand
        and fan it out
like a deck of cards in a high-stakes game

or open up their guilt as if it is a book
        in a foreign language
they cannot understand

one held the two corners of his guilt
        as if it was a bedsheet
he must spread over my body

as if my body was a chair
        in a house closed up for the winter
and when he walked away

he forgot his guilt           I shrug it off
        turn it over in my hands
turns out his guilt is very small

not a sheet at all
        more like a handkerchief
I shout have you forgotten something

but he's walking away whistling
        I fold it up and put it in my pocket
carry it with me           always

These difficult conversations, with both men and women, are part of the work as a feminist, part of the work of a poet. Bell Hooks wrote that whilst consciousness-raising sessions in the second wave feminism movement provided a safe space for women to speak out and to tell their stories, naming the problem, or bearing witness to it, was 'only one stage in the radical transformation' and the next step would have been 'the confrontation between women and men, the sharing of this new and radical speech: women speaking to men in a liberated voice'. Poetry can step into this space, allowing women a place to speak with authority, through the activation of the female gaze, to say 'I see you seeing me'.

# Martyn Crucefix

## The Ekphrastic Poetic Choice

**David Pollard**, *Three Artists – Parmigianino, Caravaggio, Rembrandt*
(Lapwing Publications, 2017)
**Seamus Cashman**, *The Sistine Gaze* (Salmon Poetry, 2015).
**Matthew Sweeney**, *My Life as a Painter* (Bloodaxe Books, 2018).

Two of these collections extend the ekphrastic poetic choice to book-length compositions and to the heights of achievement in the fine arts. Cashman takes on Michelangelo's work in the Sistine Chapel, while Pollard's book is divided into sections on Parmigianino, Rembrandt and Caravaggio. Initially, Pollard presents a set of 'meditations' on Parmigianino's 'Self Portrait in a Convex Mirror' (c. 1524). This is a bold move, given that John Ashbery did the same thing in 1974 and Pollard explores many similar ideas. Both writers are intrigued by a self-portrait painted onto a half-spherical, contoured surface to simulate a mirror. The viewer gazes at the painted image of a mirror in which is reflected a painted image of the artist's youthful and girlish face. It's this sense of doubling images that Pollard begins with. 'You are a double-dealer' he declares, addressing the artist directly, though the language is quickly thickened and abstracted into a less than easy, philosophical style. Such paradoxes draw the poet in: 'you allow the doublings / inherent in your task to hide themselves / in open show'.

The poems are in free verse, line endings often destabilising the sense, and lightly punctuated when I could have done with more conventional punctuation given the complex, involuted style. Pollard likes to double up phrases, his second attempt often shifting ground or seeming propelled more by sound than sense. He observes that the artist's paint is 'composed of almost nothing like words / that in their vanishings leave somewhat / of their meaning' – a 'somewhat' that falls well short of anything definitive. This again echoes Ashbery and appeals to our modern sensibility but Pollard images such a sense of loss with 'a rustle of leaves among the winds / of autumn blowing in circles / back into seasons of the turning world'. He does not possess Ashbery's originality of image, here deploying the clichéd autumnal leaves and then echoing Eliot's 'still point of the turning world'. Indeed, many of the poems are frequently allusive (particularly of Shakespearean phrases, Keats coming a close second).

The Rembrandt poems have a similar tone and style, not surprisingly when most of the focus is on the mirroring and self-reflection of his self-portraits, but the final Caravaggio section makes different ekphrastic choices. Pollard allows the artist a direct voice in one poem, considers seven individual images in others, then concludes again with something close to a 'meditation'. Those familiar with Caravaggio will recognise the play of light out of thick slabs of shadow and 'plain speech not mannered rhetoric'. Such a visual 'plain speech' is well described in 'The Entombment' in the image of Christ's 'liminal grey flesh' and, in 'The Rising of Lazarus', Caravaggio employs grave robbers to 'drag a grave' for a real, decaying corpse since 'he only painted from grit and real'. Pollard's language often has energy, but I doubt its precision in such choices as 'drag' and 'grit' – the former tries too hard, the latter not hard enough. Nevertheless, the ambition and seriousness of intent in this collection cannot be doubted.

Unlike Pollard, Seamus Cashman takes us to the moment when his single long poem began. Re-visiting the Sistine Chapel, we are told his eyes fall on a painted figure in a white, pseudo-architectural, triangular frame – a woman in a green jacket: 'Her eyes hold mine, and the word "gaze" slips into my mind. As I stare she seems to invite me to converse'. The resulting 'conversation' is the extraordinarily ambitious poem that follows, drawing on Michelangelo's work on the ceiling of the Chapel (completed in 1512) and the altar wall (completed 1541).

But the woman is hardly given a voice and the substance of the sequence is dominated by the (male) artist's reflections on his years-long task. He's found 'between this scaffold floor and ceiling', complaining about his 'craned neck', pouring plaster, crushing pigments, enumerating at great length the qualities of the paint he employs (Cashman risking an odd parody of a Dulux colour chart – 'Variety is my clarity, / purity my colour power'). These period and technical details work well, but Cashman's Michelangelo sometimes also shades interestingly into a more future-aware voice, melding – I think – with the poet's own voice. So he remarks: 'Getting lost is not a condition men like me endure or venture on today. / All GPS and mobile interlinks enmesh our every step'.

Cashman's verse has a Whitmanesque quality (the long lines) and can bring to mind Blake's Prophetic Books; it has dashes of Hopkins' alliterative energy. The voice wants 'to sing. I want to sing the body tune, / the rhythms of blood, the living heart' but I found myself wishing for less effortful transcendence and a more Traherne-like, child-like, simplicity of diction, still capable of conveying what Michelangelo declares, at a late stage, that 'our instinct is infinity'. This might also sit more comfortably with Cashman's Michelangelo's intentions which seem to be to give 'hope to some pilgrim searching my cabinet for direction and new ritual'. I think we are meant to see Cashman himself as this 'pilgrim', a latter-day man, having lost his Catholic beliefs, visiting the Chapel in search of a new vision. Certainly, the Michelangelo-voice does not speak in a confined 16th century fashion about art in praise of God, the poem instead working towards a modern – or perhaps Blakean – godless vision of human life where 'heaven is adoration of knowledge, and god is who we know ourselves to be'. So Cashman ekphrastically takes on the Sistine Chapel and proceeds to write God out of the picture. Nor does he shrink from the shelf-clearing consequences for our conventional spiritual understanding. The idea of the 'Soul' is now little more than a 'word. It frightens children and old painter sculptors weakened by the weight of brush and mallet. Soul. / Nothing knows its place'.

Matthew Sweeney's new collection, despite its title, contains few ekphrastic poems. The book's epigraph is from Frank O'Hara's 'Why I am Not a Painter' and the poems, ekphrastic or not, don't depart far from what Sean O'Brien describes as Sweeney's style of 'grim, gleeful, unrelenting fantasies'. Sweeney's facility and familiarity with his particular mode of working make the art of writing poems look deceptively easy. The odd-ball imaginative flights are full of surprises but – without getting too po-faced about it – his surreal excursions are always firmly grounded in a familiar speaking voice and a recognisably shared world. This means – unlike some forms of surrealism – he does not cut dead the more difficult facts of love, death and power (language is not one of his subjects). So in 'Iceland', the wish to holiday there is explicitly linked to 'corpses and blood-puddles' on TV: 'I need to get away, / but where do I go?' Elsewhere there are fleeting glimpses of both Barack Obama and Donald Trump (the latter as a bear – to be killed and eaten).

Also, a more personal paranoia is never too far away (a helicopter whirrs overhead, soldiers scour a shoreline) and in 'Van Gogh's Gun' the narrator accepts Don McLean's 1971 pop judgement that 'this / world was maybe not for you', but that 'this world' was precisely what Van Gogh painted, then finally concludes 'You couldn't stick it'. Sweeney's address to the painter Paula Modersohn-Becker – who died aged thirty-one soon after childbirth – is poignantly titled '*Schade!*' meaning 'What a pity!' and she interests Sweeney in being an outsider, an artist, someone hounded to her death by external forces. In fact, these poems often read to me like protective charms against pain, suffering and injustice. One protagonist goes to great lengths to purchase and install a second-hand nuclear bunker. In 'Frogman', a man has kept an absurd diving suit for which he has been roundly mocked, yet when the floods come, what looked foolish and merely eccentric, means he is now prepared: 'He looked forward to being the city's last survivor'. In 'The Old Xmas Tree', the abandoned tree is neglected in the garden, then discarded, but the narrator lies down in its place and, in a magical-real identity exchange, he dreams 'of Xmas, the presents placed under me, the gonks, cards and angels in my / branches, and me green again'.

Such part-comic redemption or self-renewal reads as particularly poignant given Sweeney's recent announcement that he is suffering from motor neurone disease. In an imagined memo to the painter L.S. Lowry, Sweeney suggests 'there are also the beautiful who, if we're lucky, save us from ourselves, and validate / The sun's light'. We should think of Sweeney in this way. In the voice of a bear and in clearly valedictory tones he assures us: 'Don't / worry, I'll have my own jar of / honey, and I'll be wearing blue / sunglasses and a porkpie hat'. The final poem presents a rite of passage and further little ritual of jazz, wine, a snake, a lizard, and a painted yellow pole stuck into a poet's grave. At the end, the pole is to be removed and the mourner is instructed to 'march to the swollen river, / arch your arm and fire the / lemon javelin into the water.'

# Patricia McCarthy

## Pilgrimage

**John F. Deane:** *Dear Pilgrim*, Carcanet, 2018

This is a major poet writing at the height of his powers. As the title suggests, John Deane invites all human beings, or pilgrims, whether Christian or not, to partake in his revelatory, redemptive collection. He stresses the importance of 'straining always/ towards fellowship'.

This strong sense of community is further highlighted in the hoarse voice of the 'old folk' who 'have gathered in our time/ such treasurable loveliness, who have stood together'. In the poem 'The Turning' his wife is out in the garden whereas he, the poet, is inside 'hearing the vole-like scritch and scratch of my biro as it turns, turns,/ to work at the daunting, cosmic whiteness of the page'. And indeed, it is this 'cosmic whiteness of the page' that Deane covers with a true cosmic poetry for all of us in all time. He is not afraid 'to relish beauty' and is 'willing to have the poem/ speak the improbable wonderful' ('An Elegy'). His poems deserve to reveal themselves slowly, on all their various levels and layers, each poem a contemplation, both secular and spiritual, that needs to be imbibed without pressure, and many times, for its full impact to come across.

It is unusual to find such a visionary poet nowadays, one so deeply rooted in his faith that there is no didacticism or sectarianism. Hopkins and Geoffrey Hill (Deane even has a 'Mercian Hymn' here to compare with Hill's) and Herbert come to mind. He understands a common anxiety: how many of us are 'scared to believe, fearful of unbelief'; the poems breathe out with purity from the poet's heart, and are firmly rooted in the natural world, 'in this earth's allelulia, its de profundis'. Different species of birds are described in such minute detail that Deane could be mistaken for an ornithologist whose extraordinarily detailed language with hitched-together adjectives recalls more specifically Gerard Manly Hopkins, and lifts each specimen and species into a painterly life to give the reader that thrill that comes from the buoyancy of the lexis. Flowers, too, both the usual and rare, are named at times almost as mantras and weave themselves lyrically into the lines with affirmation.

In many poems, one world is juxtaposed with another, or ends on a final few lines as a summary or comment on the previous lines. Deane gives the sonnet form a fresh twist, dispensing with rhyme, but the sonnet still is a frame that contains the concentration of what the poet has to say with his mix also of alliteration and extended similes.

Poetry and music are one in so many ways in this book. In 'Epithalamium' the poet, while referring to a marriage, actually subconsciously, whether he knows it or not, describes what his poems manage to do, echoing on musically into the silence: 'when the singing ends/ the song continues,// when the poem is written at last, the poetry begins'. In the memorable poem, 'The Upright Piano', a piano is loaded onto a currach in the pouring rain to take it to an island, but the boat 'lurched sideways into the reaching arms of a wave' and the piano sank – so that, 'under the rough-cast gurgling cacophonies, the gripe-words'

> ...you will hear
> the busy-fingered currents
> perform a suite
> of intricate and burble-delicate water-music.

In the Slipper Chapel, en route to Little Walsingham, the stained glass of the Annunciation window actually is the music. It is 'a 40-voice motet in blue' – too much needs quoting to demonstrate the painterly joy and affirmation in this poem 'Letter from East Anglia' which echoes near its end with 'the long reiterated litanies, humankind's// polyphony of pleas and pleading'.

John Deane is very much aware of the plight of humankind, and of man's natural inclination to doubt. He himself, like Hopkins, has doubts at times. In 'Visitation', for example he asks 'what of the all-at-once love-words of annunciation?' He thinks of the Crucifixion of Christ and universalises His suffering on the cross: 'The agonies we suffer// what of them if it is all pointless?' In 'A Mosaic' from the sequence 'Violin Concerto', he asks, with great humility, a very big question:

> ...And shall I have – after it all –
> realised anything of consequence,
>
> or added one emerald tessera
> to the star-floored dwelling-place of Yeshua incarnate?

Despite the philosophical and spiritual tenets in this collection, even if he speaks for all time, the poet remains earth-bound and based in our present day which he often views with a tempered disgust. In 'Coast' he contrasts the 'dulled and bulging' eyes of the dead fish in their boxes with 'the bulged eyes of the tourists, creatures,// out of their element, alien here and cold'. In 'The Downs, The Cedars', he imagines Christ in the suburbs with its 'cute/beribboned gardens, four-by-fours/ discreet and ostentatious, ego-sheen off chrome/ and alloy', and this original focus allows the poet to satirise all the more sharply our materialistic, irreligious age. He imagines this suburban Christ 'leafleting where he can', wonders if the feral cats rub up against his trouser legs 'as he steps cautiously round dried-up dog turds;//doors closed, alarms, no junk mail'... And he asks wryly, in a kind of summary, 'What news, then of the inner life? The postman/ whistles, bin lorries clank... politicians, thieves.../ and the Christ still labours on towards Calvary'. In 'The Whole World Over', set in Budapest, the poet's revulsion with 'the ego-wassailing of flesh' and 'the slippery/ eel-mud of the mind' is accentuated even more and brings to mind Yeats' 'foul rag and bone shop of the heart'. Interestingly, in this collection, unlike perhaps some of his earlier collections, John Deane avoids directly confronting politics; in fact here he holds back even from tackling politics from what Heaney said is the only way to do so – 'at an angle'.

As might be expected, he deals as easily as John Burnside does with the afterlife and those gone before us. In 'As the Stars in Heaven', in which he invokes and quotes fragments from Hopkins, he urges us to gain strength from those who have gone before:

They are out there,
ghosts of the prophets and the hosts, presences of an immense
and active happiness, urging our part

in the labouring of the universe towards fruition.

Again, in 'The World is Charged', the title being a quotation from Hopkins, in taking in all the details from the natural scene about him – the cock pheasant, the Japanese anemone, the briars, the tiny pimpernel, the ragwort, woodlouse, eucalyptus, owl, and the stars above – Dean is super-aware of all the levels and layers of generations who have lived, loved, worked and vanished 'into the deep, where they stay// resonant in their silence, their poorer cottages crumbled/ into liqueur of rose hip, dust of nettle, knowing that we too/ will be with them, alive and loving, in the warm light/ that still persists, hereabouts, and everywhere, and forever'. Likewise, in the very moving elegy to his brother, 'The Great Fire' we are aware of those who have gone before:

... all they have achieved
lies hidden, in that particle of star-being, that fleck of ash
from the great fire, that has been their flesh

– a sadness perhaps that, with faith or without, all comes to nothing.

In the extraordinarily moving, musical and delicate rendering of the Middle English poem, *Pearl*, that surely even surpasses the award-winning well-handled version by Jane Draycott, the daughter, the 'pearl', appears from the afterlife to the father, to his passionate delight, and reassures him that she is still with him even though she is in heaven. He must wait, she says: 'wait in hope, till all the twigs and branches/grow into the blessed, the sacred and eternal tree'.

> 'My being', she said, 'is Hallelujah,
> And all my fire Hosanna'.

There are many fine illuminating treasures in this long dramatic poem, ending with the father coming out of his dream/sleep, finding in his palm a large, living pearl which he raises to his mouth 'where it melted slowly' on his tongue – just like the communion wafer: 'and I was fed by it, and my thirst was quenched'.

As has already been seen, this collection is in no way insular; it encompasses all time, and many places such as Ireland, England, Israel and Palestine, yet never once stoops to being touristy. In the beautifully achieved sonnets in the sequence 'According to Lydia', the persona is an unknown female disciple of Christ and through her authentic account we see with fresh eyes a new testament that unrolls filmically and as powerfully, but much more positively with the grace of its language and images, as the priest's haunting sermons in Joyce's *Portrait of the Artist as a Young Man*.

In the last sonnet, 'Lydia', it is as if the main images in this book come together in a final, meaningful orchestral chord, similarly to the way T S Eliot's images in the *Four Quartets* evolve symbolically until 'the fire and the rose are one':

> Do not fear, he said, only
> believe. I work to keep the heart open, glory in the once-fire
> that will be ash, in reason beyond reason. I work to cherish
> the variegated birdsong, the damson flowers blossoming
> when they will. That I might overflow with Yeshua...

And isn't it just this that John F. Deane does with his own poetry in this book?

# Martin Caseley

## Lines Converging Towards the Cloud of Unknowing: the Poetry of James Harpur

i

James Harpur's latest collection, *The White Silhouette,* continues his visionary exploration of several themes evident throughout his poetic career, but they are in many ways culminations of his familiar concerns, rendered with greater precision, freedom and authority.

When Harpur's first collection, *A Vision of Comets* appeared from Anvil Press in 1993, some of these perennial themes were already evident. 'Revised Myth', for instance, is his first exploration of St. Patrick casting out snakes in Ireland; rather than an exercise in local colour. However, Harpur depicts the snakes morphing into an ouroboros-type symbol which 'lies waiting, swelling under the thin skin of the New Testament', a challenge to modern sanctity and a troubling subterranean presence still beneath the Irish landscape.[1] The poem begins with a passage of physicality and energy reminiscent of Ted Hughes, but ends with something more worrying and inconclusive: 'waiting for the saints on St. Peter's/ to drop off one by one', when it will presumably re-emerge, surfacing with the violence of Tennyson's Kraken.

Harpur is also much exercised by the historic witness of faith through the ages, whether that be transmitted in the form of buildings, iconography or the individual testimonies of saints and other figures. Another poem from his first volume, 'Tithe Barn at Bradford on Avon', depicts the building as a chthonic creature, 'bricks like the tarnished scales/ of a fabulous medieval monster'. In this earthy context, like a sudden revelation from a fable, shines the contrast of a cruciform shape, 'like molten silver', but it is given real definition only by the 'sodden mould'. The historical context and importance of paying the tithe is perhaps emphasised by Harpur's description of the building as 'alone' and still suffused with 'blackness', rather than recollecting its harvest role. It is the sort of outline found lurking in the background of Samuel Palmer paintings, growing into the dark

---

[1] Harpur's publications are: *A Vision of Comets (1993), The Monk's Dream (1996), Oracle Bones (2001), The Dark Age (2007), Angels and Harvesters (2012)* and *The White Silhouette (2018)*. All are published by Anvil, except the last, which is by Carcanet Press. All quotations in the body of this essay are from these respective volumes, unless otherwise footnoted.

shadows, rather than glowing like the innocent parishioners[2]. The cruciform shape is 'branded' into it violently: this is no unruffled picture of medieval community.

Exploring faith and religious belief, Harpur often uses dramatic monologue, gradually building a gallery of scriptural and clerical figures: in this volume, 'Samson' and 'Christ and the Woman of Samaria' being two notable examples. In the former, Samson, in the act of destroying the temple columns, prays urgently for strength, but also for vision and resurrection: 'let me rise into your kingdom', he begs, 'my eyes healed, blinded by your glory rising'. 'Christ and the Woman of Samaria' is more orthodox, setting up a fairly obvious contrast between physical drought and the spiritual water offered by Christ's words. In both poems, there are vivid details – Samson's muscles 'slither like rats' under his skin, the Samaritan woman's life is compared to an empty water jug – but there is not yet something truly compelling in the form. The disturbing intensity of the tithe barn and the ambiguity raised in retelling myth are not yet wedded to clear, indivual voices.

Three years later, in *The Monk's Dream*, 'Lazarus' offers a considerably more ambitious retelling of a familiar Biblical episode. 'Memories stiffen in my bones', the speaker confesses early on, and the attentions of Martha and Mary offer a restrained sense of sick-room domesticity as they nurse the dying man. Ironically, he outlives them, but remembers 'unravelling into light' and 'a release from pressured flesh'. The Christ appears in a welter of clashing images and oxymorons: the crowd, waiting, are 'confident with doubt', whilst Lazarus himself realises the dangers: 'If I had got too near his darkened soul/ I knew I would have been obliterated'. Commanded to return to his physical body, Lazarus is at first unwilling: 'a compulsion to escape coursed through me', he recalls, then afterwards 'the anger came' from the ignorant witnesses, until eventually he is reduced to 'an anecdote/ the butt of jokes'. Jesus, 'the young rabbi', weeps, disturbed 'because he had to sacrifice/ a soul released from flesh', but Lazarus understands the nature of the miraculous. The nature of his continued existence is, however, more problematic: 'soon my practised answers/ encrusted my soul like rust' and his life becomes 'a rehearsal/ for an event/ which had already happened.' The story also offers Harpur the chance to explore later ramifications after this incident, which he resisted in the earlier monologues. The transformed lives of Martha and Mary are balanced against 'the roads lined with carrion

---

[2] See, for example, the contrast between the church spire and the gilded surroundings in Palmer's *The Magic Apple Tree*, or the treatment of the church buildings in *Coming from Evening Church* (both 1830).

bound to crosses.' The speaker himself, however, bears the greatest weight: he is 'always at one remove from experience' and he concludes with some bitterness 'after I died/ I never lived again.' Here the contradictory impulses of a gospel parable (strength v. weakness, life v. death) are not left merely as dramatic oppositions – instead they vividly galvanise and inhabit the troubled character of the speaker.

'The Road to Westport', a long account of climbing Croagh Patrick, introduces the recurring motif of pilgrimage in Harpur's work. The poem itself sees him revisit both the St. Patrick myth and the location of an earlier poem, 'Climbing Mount Patrick', but here the visionary aspects of the experience are explored at greater length and taken a step further. The bodily aches of climbing are brushed aside – 'I watch the heads of pilgrims/ lead their bodies into view' – when clouds part and Ireland is suddenly glimpsed 'like a distant mottled Canaan'. The poet retraces his steps to ground level, but is granted a visionary glimpse of 'a white-cloaked congregation' of saints associated with Irish myth and legend, gathered there 'to bless the seamless country'. The previous poem included glimpses of other pilgrims making this harsh climb, but vouchsafed 'no voice of God... no burning bush.'

Just as this volume takes its title, *The Monk's Dream*, from a famous medieval incident foretelling a king's death, the following one, *Oracle Bones*, is titled after a poem about the preparations for auguring success on a similar hunt: the king will be successful because 'the moment is in joint' and the requisite cosmic pressures are in harmony. 'Retired Augur' reanimates one of those left behind by the coming of the age of reason: the voice of one who can read the ever-changing pattern protests that 'the point is beauty – not divine communication', before the deadening 'predetermined meaning' is flung over it. The parallels with poetry are obvious; however, there is a cultural place for such foretellings - 'let the rituals stagger on', he suggests, 'as stabilising pageantry', but the rational law also favours punishments such as crucifixion, which will ironically guarantee 'a thousand years of peace'. Such inhumanity is often rationalised in this way.

Harpur here shows a much more sophisticated grasp of the gyres of history and cultural shifts than in the earlier Bible tales he took as source material. The speaker in 'The Assyrian Extispicist' shows a more cynical awareness of his power: 'should truth emerge in clarity... then temper it with doubtful words', he comments, like a voice from one of Browning's 'Men and Women'. 'The Delphic Priest', however, hears the grinding of changing cultural gears: 'our time had gone', he ruefully notes, whilst 'the new myth enters silently/ in woods and subterranean streams/ a whisper in the budding shoots/ in voices, oracles and dreams'. The voices of creation are 'fragments of a broken poem' and those pieces often illuminate the lost voices of those who would have recognised themselves as men and women of faith, even if it is not a faith we would easily recognise today.

A gallery of Irish saints recurs in *The Dark Age*, Harpur's fourth volume, and once again there is a poem celebrating Patrick: 'Patrick's Return', however, celebrates creation as evidence of God's love. The 'yearning for release' sensed by Patrick at the beginning of the poem is a direct paraphrase of Romans 8:19, referring to the revelation of God's children: Patrick's prayer releases this revelation with a direct simplicity missing from the equivocating augurs. Explorations of Fintan, Fursey and other Irish saints are, however, much darker: 'trophy heads' of soldiers are brought to the former, whilst the latter, scarred as a witness and as a penance, warns 'pilgrims who seek the furnace in my cell' that he sees 'two trapdoors into hell'. Elsewhere in this collection, St. Simeon Stylites watches from his pillar the 'sundial of the Lord': injured, emptied of his sense of self, he becomes suffused with love, purifed by being 'drowned/ in the paralysis of light'. Watching men about their purposeful, burdensome business like so many ants, he realises 'each one of them is Christ', a mute, detached witness, a 'pillar of stillness' in his extremity.

This volume also includes Harpur's first two explorations of the Book of Kells, the illuminated 9th Century gospel manuscript which he would later revisit. 'Verbum' contains credo-like advice: 'leave the road of affirmation/ the road of thinking and imagining/ just be a pilgrim to yourself' and, later, 'just watch your convoluting self.' The other Kells poem, 'Scribe B', advises self-denial with the abbot's words to the scribe 'You are God's medium/ he does not want your thought'. Taken together, these poems exult in anonymity and advise a kind of unreflecting mindlessness – both difficult paths for the poet to follow.

Harpur returns to the Book of Kells in both his fifth and his latest collections, prompting a rich series of encounters and meditations. In *Angels and Harvesters*, the actual first physical encounter between the poet and the book is dramatised. The poem, entitled 'On First Seeing the Book of Kells' proposes an encounter charged with as much meaning as Keats' 'On First Looking Into Chapman's Homer'. Just as Keats feels he has encountered 'a new planet' or when 'stout Cortez' surveys the Pacific with wonder, Harpur (after undercutting the scene with everyday bathos) responds 'I'm looking at a dream... or a blueprint/ of creation' as the script on vellum flares into life and colour before him. Making sense of the illuminated initials on the manuscript, he reels: 'Where is the Word? And what's this world...' Lingering, like one decoding a 'magic eye' picture, he blurs the focus until he can read the latin *in Principio erat Verbum* (in the beginning was the Word), the first words of John's gospel. For poets, of course, the translation and transmission of the word carries innumerable connotations, but here Harpur solely concentrates on decoding the decorated, cartoonish letters, commenting approvingly on how they appear 'pristine and freed' – in later poems, he will explore the extraordinary genesis and transmission of such a document, but at this point, recalling Cortez and Keats, he is content to gaze upon a new-found land in wonder.

ii

*'The White Silhouette'* (Carcanet, 2018) continues to explore these themes of pilgrimage, belief and history, but brings some of them to what feels like a definitive statement. There is a new and different personal note to the poems exploring belief and a historical focus on religious objects; the Book of Kells, a supreme example of this, remains an inspiration to Harpur, but now he utilises his gift for monologue to animate the anonymous scribes and how we encounter their work today. The attractions of pilgrimage as a process of spiritual growth remain evident, but personal encounters, sometimes of the most raw biographical sort, are seen to mediate the asceticism sometimes demanded.

'The Journey East', the poem which opens the book, suggests some of these new spaces: ostensibly a car journey undertaken from Ireland to Somerset, it assumes the reader is alert to the playfulness of Biblical parallels. Three are journeying, following stars, it is the advent season, the Somerset Levels, when encountered, are 'crisp and even', woodsmoke is 'incense', curtains are 'gold' and arrival is greeted by 'a star that's stopped overhead'. The poem boasts a glitter of proper names – Severn, Yeovil, Cattistock – but it's clear that arrival is merely the beginning. For a more personal account of spiritual searching and eventual revelation, the reader must turn to the title poem, 'The White Silhouette', whilst noting that a silhouette is merely an outline.

In 'The White Silhouette', Harpur gently mocks his own preconceptions for meeting a mysterious pilgrim: no revelatory meeting takes place in the quiet piety of George Herbert's church, nor John's island-cell of Patmos, nor, interestingly, in timeless, rural Ireland. Despite his 'upright praying disposition' it is not until he turns to 'meditation and prayer', 'accumulating quietude' in a domestic setting that he begins to glimpse mystical certainty. Even resignation and the dolours of the negative way cannot further his search: poems sent up like distress flares eventually bring self-knowledge. 'All I have to do is stay/ where I am, ready to be rescued' he realises, losing his self-conscious identity and merging into the one who was 'too close to home' all along. Rather than waiting for 'something to ignite', he must invest himself in 'a camouflaged prayer/ dispatched towards the Cloud of Unknowing.' English mysticism helps him to name this: 'The Song of Richard Rolle', author of 'The Cloud of Unknowing', a poem in *Angels and Harvesters*, considers 'holy fire' and loud songs to 'wake the saints', yet ultimately these subside into an image of fervent, powerful prayer. In both poems there is a tuning – or attuning, in its metaphysical sense[3] – before the correct form of music can be heard or produced. 'The White Silhouette' concludes, mysteriously affirming the Trinity, with 'I you us' merging into 'Iesus', the word becoming flesh in another sense.

Harpur's poetic dialogue with the Book of Kells continues, evidenced by four long pieces in the central section of this book. Having encountered the physical presence of the book and wondered at its survival and beauty, Harpur now creates a long monologue, 'Goldsmith', giving what TV scriptwriters call the 'back story' of one of the anonymous scribes, named after his use of yellow and blue colours. He is one amongst many pilgrims, seeking 'shimmering shrines' on Iona, struggling to capture Christ on vellum for the ages. The abstract 'formlessness' he agonises over eventually emerges as the trust that 'painting incarnates the spirit' and the image will emerge from the vellum, similar to how a sculpted shape emerges from being hidden in a lump of stone. The pure Idea becomes 'a flow of energeia/ destroying the veil between seer and seen' – what is required is simply discernment (or perhaps Blakean perception). In the following poem, the poet meditates on 'Scribe B' in the Irish Library of Monaco, a strangely contrasting setting where 'it's always noon'. Back in Kells, years before, the poet is 'in search of home', but realises that he is really tracking an 'idea of ruined choirs'; coming to Iona, Scribe B also seeks validation, but through his handiwork. 'My heart burns for praise', he admits, but symbolically pours his lifeblood into his lettering, mingling 'rage, grief, immortality', a frank depiction of all-too-human vanity. The third Kells poem, 'Gerald of Wales', explores the contradictions of 'sacred art': angels in dreams offer visionary vistas of saints and monks leading to the Blakean edict, 'Imagination is nothing but/ the recollection of the holy'. This leads to a visit to the book, where the vellum is likened to 'the surface of a pond'. From the hidden depths emerge both dangerous voices of temptation and 'golden lines' which are 'the grace notes of a harp'. Ambition frustrated, Gerald finds himself in Lincoln, looking back at missed opportunities: 'within the vellum of that book/ lines sprouted like destinies/ I'd missed, rejected or ignored.' This poem concludes with a definition of the beauty of the visionary moment: 'a moment, unrepeatable', electrical in its ferocity, but the images need the

---

[3] See, famously, Donne's use of this image in 'Hymne to God, my God, in My Sicknesse'.

medium of the page, existing only for it, to allow 'the enormity of something Other' to leak through: once again, parallels with a world of Blakean forms and archetypes suggest themselves here.

The last of the four Kells poems returns to John 1.1, as already celebrated in Harpur's earlier description of his first encounter with the book: it incorporates the whole of the earlier poem, but builds a further context around it. The book is a living thing, as the letters 'start to surface' – once again, from some submerged area within or below the vellum – 'the book proclaims the Gospel/in words as unambiguous as light/ and yet the concert of its patterns suggests/reality as sinuous flux'. Later, contemplating, Harpur realises 'the process/ is the crux' to transformative art, conferring 'a temporary grace/ that's like an anamnesis/ of life's peregrinal venture'. The final image in the poem returns to the idea of converging lines, but the lines of a tapestry rather than a book, with the perfect, ordered pattern only seen from one side: 'we see our pattern in brocaded glory'.

Other ways these patterns persist are shown in the sequence entitled 'Graven Images', each slim poem describing a surviving fragment of religious statuary, engraving or stained-glass fragment. Formally and tonally different to the longer, more rhetorical Kells poems, these for me are the real surprises of this volume, being exercises in concision and directness.

On the page, these are ten brief, Giacometti-slim pieces celebrating the fractured fragments that survived iconoclasm and religious upheavals through the centuries. Paring down his sometimes prolix lines, Harpur gives us their sheer, lumpen power as reflections of belief, outlasting the violence done to them. For example, 'Bishop's Head' from Winchester Cathedral:

...left your head
to roll in the aisle,
a gargoyle
against
the goblins
of their senses.

The violence is shocking, defacing (literally) the Bishop, but the malevolence of those capable of this is worse, and a hint of gold and incense (that is, spiritual beauty and devotion) can still be ascertained behind the ruined features. The images remain charged with their transformative grace and power down through the centuries. 'Broken' describes a crucifix figure thus: 'chesspiece/king/ arms snapped from thorax/stick legs/head sunk', patterning later violence onto unavoidable echoes of the Passion of Christ. In some cases, these representations of holy art have the power to leap clear of several historical contexts. A meditation on a life-size dead Christ, discovered post-war, 'Wounds', describes how the shocking violence depicted outlasts falling bombs and postwar clearance, remaining somehow out of time and vivid. The final poem in this sequence, 'Glass', suggests that reinterpreting such fragments is an imaginative act, the mysterious power of such shards of beauty only just below the vellum surface. Like the Kells poems, this is an imaginative encounter, reinterpreting these images of power and grace through the thin, attenuated lines of poetry, but this sequence seems a considerable achievement.

Where might Harpur go from here? The exploration of texts and fragments surviving to give witness of faith could be a worked seam and might be over. One or two of the other, self-contained poems in this volume suggest that a new, more personal angle on pilgrimage may be evolving. 'The Summer World' and 'Portora Royal' hint at more personal peregrinations: the former is a school memory, suffused with a sense of loss in an exam summer, on the verge of setting out. The latter returns to a 'last family holiday', mixing the banal, the touching and the adolescent's sense of distance. These are very different, self-consciously foregrounding ordinary detail, both subtitled 'from *In Loco Parentis*', but, although affecting and convincing as poems, the use of anecdotal memories brings different tensions and challenges. It will be interesting to see if Harpur can find sufficient grace-notes and numinous intimations swimming beneath the surface of the personal.

# Gerald Dawe

**Derek Mahon**: *Against the Clock* (Gallery Press, 2018)

In 'A Bangor Requiem', Derek Mahon's poem on the death of his mother, he recalls a neighbourhood 'of bay windows and stiff/ gardens shivering in the salt sea air, / the sunburst ideogram on door and gate, / you knew the secret history of needlework, / bread-bin and laundry basket awash with light, / the straight-backed chairs, the madly chiming clock'.

'A Bangor Requiem', part of the epic-like *The Yellow Book* sequence, along with *The Hudson Letter* sequence (retitled *New York Time*), marks an opening out of Mahon's poetic form into a much more conversational tone close to the canto-like control of Louis MacNeice's *Autumn Journal*. Not so much laid-back as meditative, self-reflective and expansive and calling attention to the corporate language and cultural diction of late 20th and early 21st centuries. Notice in the above extract the visual detail which brings a social world into view but also 'the madly chiming clock'.

In his mother's house her way of life is passing yet retains these symbols which are also functioning, actual 'things' – bread bin, laundry basket. Things which also feature in the great 17th century Dutch artists Mahon has praised in poems – most famously in 'Courtyards in Delft' – for their astute literal imaginations capable of transforming what is real and present, the here and now, with a sense of radiance. Wait a while and look, the poems suggest; spend time seeing and paying attention to the real; forget the endless hungering of the ego for recognition and confirmation. To sound slightly evangelical about it all, the ordinary produces its own mystery and depth benefitting attention, the draw of the imagination.

In his most recent collection, *Against the Clock*, Mahon has gone a step further and created a book of poems which can be read as a continuous complete meditation on the passing of time, the act of writing and the structure of feelings underlying both. While Tu Fu, Montaigne and Kierkegaard, among others, inhabit the poems, in this his most Yeatsian book to date, shaping it all there is, to my mind at least, the sound or presence of the great 18th century writer, Samuel Johnson. His intelligence and humanistic imagination finds philosophical echoes throughout this sonorous, challenging and important collection. Everything is relative and deftly handled, in the resurgent six-line stanzas for starters, like the image of the clock against which time is measured but yet also furnishes a life being lived, honoured, enjoyed. The pleasure of being is the pleasure of seeing things through as in 'A Birthday' addressed to the poet's daughter:

And now you're forty (phew!), yourself a mum,
a 'single mother' since your gentil knight
was roughly carried off into the night
leaving you a widow; but when you come
to visit, the wise child is there once more
if older and slightly wiser than before.

What can I wish for you but happier days
to make up for the crisis you came through
with such resilience? Always here for you,
I watch your life unfold in phases, always
picturing that maid in a flowery smock,
whose recent photo rests against the clock.

The last phrase, pointing literally to a photograph resting 'against the clock', picks up the title-poem's 'writing against the clock' with its concluding injunction, 'we're obliged to stick it out/ until the pen falls from the trembling hand; / so just get on with it'.

Elsewhere in the collection poems sparkle with idiomatic sense and sensibility ('So face the brave new world with a wry grin/ of tolerant irony, not with impotent hate'), reassurances, and a kind of elegiac celebration as in one of the finest poems in the volume, 'A North Light', in tribute to 'a great original', the powerful and singular Northern Irish visual artist, Basil Blackshaw (1931-2016):

He evidently enjoyed a whiff of sulphur
As those artists do who want to suffer
And reach the naked rim of raw creation
With everything in hard-won resolution.

Running throughout *Against the Clock*, in almost Austin Clarke-like fashion, there are the figures of classical art and fable such as Orpheus, Daphne and Eurydice, but they and their landscapes sit alongside 'Triad for Shane MacGowan' and the immediate locale of Mahon's pad in County Cork as well as the 'bedlam of acquisitive force/ that rules us and would rule the universe' of 'Trump Time'. *Against the Clock* reminds us of just how much Mahon has contributed to a humane and dynamic literary discourse about what matters in the world and how we can best survive the darkening waves which sometimes look set to engulf great art, decency and reason.

# Patricia McCarthy

## Ekphrastic Approaches

**William Bedford**: *Chagall's Circus* (Dempsey & Windle, 2019)
**Carol Rumens**: *Bezdelki: Small things*, illustrations by Emma Wright (Emma Press, 2018)
**Maitreyabandhu**: *A Cézanne Haiban* (Smith/Doorstop Books, 2019)
**Anthony Costello**: *I Freeze, Turn to Stone: The Poems of Vincent Van Gogh* (Poetry Salzburg Pamphlet series No 29, 2018)

In this collection, an ekphrastic gem, William Bedford departs from his usual bucolic vignettes set in the England of his childhood – such as in his previous impressive collections *The Fen Dancing, The Bread Horse*. Here in a series of dramatic monologues, he gets inside the mind and spirit of Marc Chagall to produce, in a wonderfully assured voice, poems focused on paintings that involve art, politics, history and of course the life of the great painter himself. The rhythm, steady throughout, accentuates the fact that the one persona, Chagall, speaks as he evolves chronologically through his life.

The book is carefully constructed to guide the reader into Chagall's paintings at different periods of his life so that, in reading the sequence, the reader is taken into an unusual art gallery. Each poem's title is that of a Chagall painting, the images are there yet there is an added dimension: Chagall himself is actually speaking to us and we gain information about his life, his influences and opinions while we look. A unique experience. The guide is clear; the groups of paintings are hung in different galleries, if you like, under headings: Russia, the Early Years: 1887-1910; The Paris Years: 1910-1914; War and Revolution in Russia: 1914-1923; France and America: 1923-1948; and The Late Work: 1948-1985. The research is obvious.

Very skilfully, Bedford brings out the character of Chagall as he weaves in images from the paintings so that the poems have many layers. The first poem from the first section, 'Self-Portrait with Brushes', delineates the artist's poverty-stricken Jewish childhood, the simple language of the young artist being conjured in the refrain *'My name is Chagall and my purse is empty'*. He 'longed for skies and stars/ but in Vitebsk there was only Vitebsk'. Even here, Bedford shows the young artist's typical dreamy, almost surreal vision in such images as the father's silence compared to:

… a forest of imagined flowers
like the cow sleeping on the roof of our barn,
the fiddler leading the bride to her wedding.

In the second poem, 'Grandfather's House' (1923), where the mother warns him of 'the hunger hiding in colours', further insights are added:

I spent my childhood devouring horizons,
seeing angels in the pattern of a carpet,
spring rain waltzing in the hessian curtains.

The painter's love for his family comes across: his mother giving birth to his younger brother, his grandfather more ambitious and visionary that his beloved father who 'all his years, lifted heavy barrels' but who had the most arresting smile:

It blew in with the cries of hunting owls,
footprints of angels on the dewed grass,
cobwebs of moonlight in the village lanes.

It is these 'bright angels', not dissimilar from Rilke's angels, that the artist vows to 'follow where they lead' him, along with acrobats, fiddlers, circus clowns. And in this collection, we track his progress through the 'world's magic' via similar translucent images that serve, for us the readers, as word-paint. In Paris he mixes with artists such as Gaugin, Kandinsky, Van Gogh and Matisse, for his 'art needed Paris as much as a spring tree needs water'. Here his work progresses: 'The Louvre was inside my head. Montmartre/ and the sun-rising Paris that never dies'. He disliked Impressionism and Cubism, and befriended Blaise Cendrars. It was not all magic, though, as the Russian revolution came with 'Nobody sane' and this brutal insanity is juxtaposed by Bedford with Chagall's earlier harmless admission that his art was that of a 'lunatic' or of 'madness' – because, presumably, it did not fit into any prevailing 'ism'. Also, in a later poem, 'The Large Circus (1968)', where he declares 'I paint poetry', Bedford shows more horrors behind many of the paintings:

The year I painted *The Large Circus*,
they shot students on an American campus.

Though using the medium of words, Bedford handles very well how Chagall disliked words, most of all poetry in his 'topsy-turvy world that needs no words'. In 'Bella with White Collar (2017)', Bedford has Chagall say:...'I refused to call my paintings poetry./ I refused to call my paintings anything.' In 'The Birthday (1915)', we see how words, for him, are not themselves, but of a different order:

The paint speaks for itself, our seventh heaven,
rainbows on canvas our way of saying grace.

With the beloved, he is lifted into 'rainbows of colour', her 'words' are his 'hand'. Together they fly 'to imaginary clouds' though the real world intrudes, for: 'Outside the waiting tractors leak red oil./ The Kulaks queue for bread. The children cry'.

Bedford shows Chagall as becoming understandably even more cynical about words in 'The Falling Angel (1923-47)' where '*Mein Kampf* and *Das Capital*' are 'squashing space':

Try words, words, words. There are no words.
Eternal blether, crushing the crushed heart.

The Fascists seem the same; they 'wear the same uniforms./ eyes blind as tombstones/ mouths squeaking in the gutters'.

It is interesting that love prevails in the penultimate poem 'Couple on a Red Background (1983)' with Chagall at last allowing a 'name' or a word, rather than a brush-stroke:

Stalin fiddling with his black moustaches,
Hitler saluting the gods in his mind.
My new beloved is Russian woman:

Her name is Valentine Brodsky,
Her name my only need of words
as heaven's gates open.

His second wife, Vava, as he called her. How wonderfully life-affirming.

All in all, this is a remarkable enlightening and enlightened sequence, an outstanding success as both a long poem, and an ekphrastic, narrative sequence. In fact, in its intricate, compelling originality, it almost defies definition. I wish I could quote from it at much greater length. In a fairly early poem, 'Red Nude Sitting Up (1908)', the Chagall we come to know in the poems says it was 'my first encounter with my own rapture'. This book expands to enable every reader to encounter rapture.

\*

There is nothing small about Carol Rumens' chapbook, *Bezdelki: Small things*, illustrated in pen and ink by Emma Wright (The Emma Press, 2018). It is a tiny book stapled together, but it has the impact of a substantial wide-ranging volume, demonstrating Rumens' musicality, originality and her erudition lightly worn. In it she summons a whole cosmos that is anywhere and everywhere, involving life and death concomitantly, suggesting that death isn't merely loss. It is effective, too, how, in such an intense rush of poetry, the illustrations, with their smudges and fine lines, allow the reader to pause and to reflect; they somehow go with the poems, without being obviously or directly connected to them. No surprise, then, that *Bezdelki* won the 2018 Michael Marks Award.

The very moving elegies and translations – mainly of Mandelstam who inspires some of Rumens' own poems – are written in memory of Yuri Georgievich Drobyshev, her late partner. They involve classical myths, many cultures, different religions, and they approach bereavement nearly always at a very oblique angle which makes them all the more moving and tender. In the four-line poem, 'At Four Months, Mind, no Requiem' the one straight-forward cry resounds in the two monosyllabic words that end the second and last lines 'lack' and 'back': 'From anywhere/ As monstrous as you like, come back!' Here, the poet, tears off her armour of dealing with her partner's death, as in the other poems, and the cry is urgent, raw, elemental. According to Catholic liturgy, the Requiem mass should have been held a month after the departed's funeral, but it still hasn't taken place.

The poet herself is, in the poem 'Equipped', in a 'thoughtfully furnished afterlife', finding a certain freedom in the pointless things (small things?) she could now do,: 'I could re-thread a strimmer/ I could drill holes in concrete', upon which her thoughts turn to ancient Egypt and the Egyptian royals in their mummy cloths 'wakeful/ in their scratchy bandages'. The shabti – wooden, stone, or faience figurines, in the form of mummies, placed in an ancient Egyptian tomb to do any work that the dead person might be called upon to do in the afterlife – are imagined here as waiting for their commands to work on a new irrigation system initiated by 'his Lordship'. The last part of the poem moves from the first person voice to the third person and the girl finds what she is doing pointless: she puts down 'the make-up slate' she is trying to find which is 'heaped with her living colour', and her deep, tender feelings flood to the surface in the last verse where the language, like the emotion, becomes purified, simple:

There's one warm face she still mirrors,
one fluid look, one undemanding smile.
She wonders about him. She tries
not to think he's out there somewhere,
being sad for her, or perhaps beyond being sad.

This poem – where the 'I' could be the poet or an anonymous person, likewise the girl described in the third person – demonstrates how successful elegies, like Thomas Hardy's 1912-13 poems, coming from a personal source, expand beyond themselves to become anyone's experience, and in this way universal.

In 'He Drank to Naval Anchors' the 'small things' in her memory of him assume the power to re-create him in couplets:

He drank to beer-bottle-tops and to hermaphrodite bread-bags,
half brown paper, half crisp cellophane

and the poem continues in a kind of mantra as he drinks to 'bison stock-cubes and Ardennes duck pâté' also 'to spattered Reeboks and to chain-store sweaters/with Pure Wool XL labels' – so the list continues, anchoring him back in reality. The last couplet repeats the first which gives him an amazing solidity.

Rumens very successfully juxtaposes such modern images as those just mentioned with ancient ones – as in the 'skinny-dipping' of the very well achieved long poem, 'King Taharqa's Last Thoughts' we are back in the ancient world (690-664 BCE) of the Nubian Pharaoh at the end of his life, after his defeat by the Assyrian armies under Esarhaddon, inspired by information on one of the surviving stelae. Perhaps the poet here is thinking how when someone dies, they may as well have lived in any age and in any century; thus she goes back and forth in time and ranges geographically very wide. The imagery is startling and there is too much to quote, but to give a flavour: the river that 'sings the shape of herself' is 'marsh-maker, rock-sucker, sky-mirror,/ word-weaver, choked with papyrus'… and then – the language becoming reminiscent of Gerard Manley Hopkins with its hitched-together words and sibilance – as it 'races the lion man's racing.' it becomes

foam-fleck, foot-flash, rainbow-flake, two of us neck-and-neck,
slipping past settlements, slopping in rock-pools, black
and white in crash-sites, slow and snakeskin-yellow
through Memphis into hundred-gated Thebes

Ghosts and souls that are always feminine, and Charon, 'the people-smuggler' who takes souls to the Otherworld are woven into the poems, as are Russian words (the 'small things' again) summoning Yuri before us. Subtle literary references also co-exist, for example to Gogol in the poem 'Vidua' with its lovely play with sounds, and to *King Lear* in the second poem 'Bezdelki with Morphine' where, like Lear putting the glass to Cordelia's mouth to see if she is still breathing, Rumens does likewise only to find that there is 'no little answering pull' and he has just died. Love survives for 'shades, you know, are kissable', and he is still alive to her as he exchanges 'small jokes' with the ferryman before she watches all the small things – his unfinished yoghurt that she eats up, the spoons and sheets she washes , even the clouds – turning into him.

The wide, piercing range of these poems is exemplified in the two quotations that preface the sequence: '*Bread, beer, oxen, birds, my heart being/sweet... cause me to carry you to anything* – from Taharqa's Prayer to Amun-Ra, and '*The soul's a woman, you know, the small things matter*' – from 'When Psyche-life...' by Osip Mandelstam. These two quotations are skilfully woven into some of the poems, so that they become part of the actual text, and serve as echoes, drawing the reader back to those very small things – like Yuri's 'tool-shed he called' his 'Jewish box', and his fur hat or 'shapka' in the perfectly executed poem, 'Shapka and Spider'('the deep-crowned cap you'll never wear – /what grave is shallower than this?'). Here, in two sestets, in blank verse and each with the same rhyme scheme ababba, she is reminiscent in tone and structure of Emily Dickinson.

The last three lines in the sequence from the poem, 'Nant y Garth' fittingly and movingly summarise the whole chap-book:

I could no more believe the sap insensible
than I believe the dead are broken branches,
and all their self-songs censored or extinguished.

\*

Maitreyabandhu's *A Cézanne Haibun* is a complete contrast to *Chagall's Circus*. Both are obviously ekphrastic yet come from different angles. Here in the haibun, with its own distinct form, there can be no dramatic monologues. Rather, the prose interspersed with short haiku-like meditations, is more of a holiday diary full of calming natural details: birds, trees, plants, winds are described in minute detail with the poet continually musing on Cézanne, quoting his sayings or dwelling on details from the latter's life such as his tricky relationship with the married Zola, and different sorts of light. Two time schemes are involved: the here and now of the prose-poet in the Sierra Aitana, and Cézanne's own epoch. The poet, Maitreyabandhu's life is also brought to the fore, unlike in *Chagall's Circus*, where Bedford is hidden in the persona of his dramatic monologues.

This seems a much less-worked long poem, more casual – and not just because it is merely stapled together. The mix of two different traditions: the haibun that originates from Japan, and the here and now travel-log of the poet's life with its ordinary down-to-earth images of wheelie bins and Tetrapacks and delicate hints at gay sex is, if nothing else, diverse. But I do feel that this is a more playful piece by Maitreyabandhu than usual. Of course, the writing has its own charm, the prose its own gentle stroll rather than a march, the musings and suppositions on Cézanne (who was most likely a secretive homosexual) are interesting little focal points for the reader but for me, personally, I didn't feel here that essential compulsion evoked by *Chagall's Circus* to read on.

Rather than being taken in an unusual way around a gallery, this little book is like a small holiday break for rest and recuperation, an amble with some culture thrown in. Yes, Cézanne has been well-researched and what seem like random biographical details of his life are well enmeshed into the prose but, for me, the force of the work is lacking.. Maybe I am unfair in comparing *A Cézanne Haibun* with *Chagall's Circus*, but, if art is, as Chagall put it, 'first and foremost a condition of the soul' then it is *Chagall's Circus – and Bezdelki: Small things* – that demonstrates this, and, fine as it may be, perhaps by the limitations of its very form, not the haibun.

*

Anthony Costello's *I Freeze, Turn to Stone: The Poems of Vincent Van Gogh* is yet another different take on ekphrastic poetry. These are found poems, transformed from Van Gogh's personal letters into achieved free verse. Found poems, for me, do carry a slight stigma, as if the person producing them ignores the considerable craft that usually goes into the composing of an original poem But the art here must be of the choosing from the prose and in making a series of moments to illuminate further Van Gogh's being, making us attend to his words differently from how we would have read them in the long flow of prose in the letters. As Helen Mort says: 'This is such an interesting and original project... *I Freeze, Turn to Stone* deepens our appreciation of the relationship between visual, written and lived experience.' The question is: whose 'poems' are they: Van Gogh's or Costello's? And has Costello been tempted to tamper a little with the passages he has picked from the letters to improve their rhythm and nuances, texture and pattern? Maybe not. Of course, they are translated – from French into English, which distances them somewhat from the original. And then 'found' poems bring up that age-old argument re free verse, and are poets just making arbitrary lines in free verse, and they would be more honest to write in prose?

Lists, such as Camille Claudel, Rodin's rejected mistress made when (wrongly) confined to an asylum for thirty plus years, abound showing not only Van Gogh's obsessiveness but also how he clings onto the normality of life, and to colours, with a certain desperation, a way of coping, particularly in the asylum. His difficulty in forming relationships is hinted at in the third last poem, 'Dear Mother':

> I have never perceived those
> to whom I have been most attached
> other than as through a glass, darkly.
> Painting is unlike anything else.

Painting, his life-saviour, solace, was his strength during his time in the asylum and after.

His panic and fear of insanity when in the asylum is shown in the poem 'Work for a Thousand Reasons': 'a more violent attack /could destroy my ability to paint'. The poem finishes with poignancy:

> I am trying to recover
> like someone who meant to commit suicide
> but makes for the bank
> because he finds the water cold.

Such confessional insights into the artist are well picked and probably what most readers would underline in going through his lengthy letters. Costello has done this for us: chosen passages of rhythm and honesty to highlight in these pages – which enable us to know the man better.

All four collections show, as Van Gogh said (Arles, August 1888), how – whether through art and/or poetry – '...life is after all almost enchanted'.

# Seán Street

From a sequence *Time and Light*:
      Poems for the Walker Art Gallery, Liverpool

## Time and Light

*The Ruins of Holyrood Chapel.*
      Louis Daguerre, oil on canvas, c. 1824

The window holds fragments of sky. Inside
there is no inside where voices that rang
flew out when unlocked acoustics turned dry,

when the vaults fell and the god was released.
What died most were the echoes – crows still call
but their songs don't ring. What sings though is light,

sound has turned now to mysteries of light
hidden and trapped, invading honest light
undramatised by glass, sun into moon

infected on contact, young light turned old
fluttering against walls, caught in rooted
webs of unresolved rafters, layered time,

vegetation where angels flew, fleeting
punctum of a flash on an altar stone
and the wound of a place's lost past healed.

He saw light impersonate sound, Time
move beyond flesh into air, how what must
be saved and salved are, in the end, shadows.

# Good Time George

*Posthumous portrait of George Melly*
Maggi Hambling, oil on canvas, 2008-9

But then you always were vibrating air,
colour pulsing – the sound the spirit has
when it's just left it to its own devices.
So hello Central get me Dr Jazz –
it's as though light flickered and you were there.


# Spring in St John's Wood

*Dame Laura Knight,* oil on canvas, c. 1933

A day it was when a beloved familiar
changing scene demanded its immortality.
Something in the light there was selected itself
to be saved, a composite essence, a moment
in North London when the season's first bustling breeze
brought neighbours out to celebrate the sanctity
of the everyday, quiet weather to preserve
against times when there is no sun, when plants die back,
cold winds blow across tennis courts, the road empties
of its voices and this light's a forgotten thing.
For now at least not so much a view as a way
of life in this part of the woods. Paint what you see
and hear. This was here and now then when the window
looked and the artist saw and drew no conclusions
because place draws its conclusions about itself.
Now when the air moves in a certain way or when
the light's right, circumstances offer suggestions.
Even now the window watches, the mind's eye sees.

# The Gods

Walter Sickert, *The Old Bedford,*
               Oil on canvas, c. 1895

A pennyworth of Heaven is all
you need, gilding to sustain the blood.
Red and gold tranced the wrapt brown and grey
lives hanging from the cliffs of the gods.

*Ladies and gentlemen, I give you*
*your own, your very own...*
Blurring reflected faces fed lust
and laughter through overwhelming light.

*The boy I love is up in the gallery.*
Not history so much as a way
of remembering, so close, so far
from us now, these bright halls, these palaces.

*Finally ladies and gentlemen*
*the orchestra, the whole company*
*but chiefly of course, yourselves!* Curtain,
and controlled eviction from the heights

out into the Jack-the-Rippered night
through pools of fluttering gas across
dark to dimly ticking terraces
and a century of wars to fight.

Long before our judgement, another
time's haunting printed on sepia,
cylinder, shellac, lore, tradition,
melting over the years to white noise.

# John Robert Lee

## Joseph and Potiphar's wife

i

'It's the coat, multi-hued, seamless,
torn off my shoulder, and torn,
torn like the rent clothes

of Israel's inconsolable grief and mourning,
that arrays anxious dreams of court intrigue
visions that recur of doors of no returning —

enslavements hold fast their rings
their vestures threaten sudden loss.

ii

Another garment spoke another lie
folded in the lonely arms
of that full-lipped, almond-eyed
Egyptian, her Midianite balm
seducing the courtyard,
the echo of her insistent psalm

of desire beating me like a hard
whip, and I ran from myself alone.'


*Art* © Richard McBee. *Joseph and Potiphar's wife*. Used with permission.


# Mythos

*'…what sacred games shall we invent.' (Nietzsche)*

# The Temple

After Mystery, myth. And the archives of our stories:
Dogon arks and Pyramid texts
cavorting gods and shape-shifting tricksters
plus Marvel's comic-book translations
with big-screen versions
Beowulf to Ragnarok to Star Wars

Mystery left to megachurches and mosques
wayside shrines and Shaker yards
vibrating crystals and palm readers —

not in those counterfeit temples of distortion
under robes of pompous priests
or teleprompting of false prophets

will we find Mystery.
Into catacombs of our death
caverns of our defeat

the horrendous abyss of failure
enters the Light of the world
and Mystery tabernacles within us.

# The Palace

Nimrod to Pharaoh to Babylonian moguls
Alexander, Caesar, holocaust butchers of the Third Reich
Asian megalomaniacs, southern caciques

variegated warlords from Genghis Khan to African tyrants
have plundered the holy places
planted standards and busts before altars of incense

recast their souls lost to Mystery
into mosaics of myth, legend and fable
doomed to lava, forest, deep-sea coral –

palace intrigues, Secret Service assassinations
Pendragon's tanks around the squares
various Orwellian oppressions

guard their mythical power.
To our sacred barricades
humble weapons of faith

anthems of love's covenants
the King comes with fierce joy
His Mystery forever triumphant.

iii

# The Town

For the hapless Town, folk-tales and superstitions
soap-operas, UFO sightings and bleeding statues
days of the dead and Nostradamus

are their credible mysteries
even as they negotiate petty dishonesties, taxes
party-politics, crime, social-media scandals

hypocrisies and complacencies
compounded now by fake news
climate disasters and mass casualties –

surely irresponsible suffrage
idolatrous political correctness
damned unbelief

have loosed ancient dragons and their beasts.
On a certain lane
near a white cedar

come visit if you like
the Carpenter's shed
to face Mystery veiled in curling shavings, sawdust.

*Art © Ken Lawrence (Saint Lucia) - "Another time". Used with permission.*
*Ken Lawrence is a Saint Lucian artist.*

# John Matthews

## The Songs of Fool

*(From a sequence of poems inspired by the 'Fool' paintings
of Cecil Collins (1908-1989)*

Fool ope'd
his heart to everything
lifted
his soul to treetops
and saw
mirrored there
his god

\*

Fool looked in the mirror
saw his soul imprisoned
broke it with his finger

blood flowed
he sobbed
O fool...

\*

Fool carried
his heart in one hand
with the other he sketched
a figure in the air
from it he took
a silver net
laid the heart within it
tossed it away

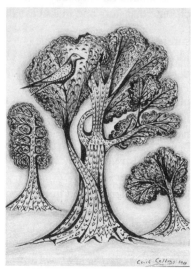

Fool saw
a goddess in the steam
waited for her to speak
she said:
Look away Fool
Fool looked away

He waited
looked back
saw her
gone.

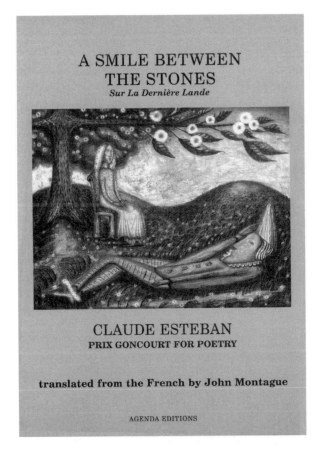

A SMILE BETWEEN
THE STONES
*Sur La Dernière Lande*

CLAUDE ESTEBAN
**PRIX GONCOURT FOR POETRY**

**translated from the French by John Montague**

AGENDA EDITIONS

These translations by John Montague, esteemed Irish poet, inspired to an extent by *King Lear,* were published by *Agenda* Editions in 2005.

Front cover: 'The Sleeping Fool,' oil on canvas 1943, by Cecil Collins. (A few copies are still available.)

# Duncan Fraser

## Ankou

Écoutez Ankou
La Mort,
avec sa faux,
his lance of stone,
and eager spade:

'Je suis La Mort
je vous tue tous – I
will
kill you
all.

I am your dark imagining –
your last desolate dream
as you stare into the obscure pit of
total erasure – I
le squelette blanc et clair,
that which remains,
sustains,
after the lambent, sensuous flesh
has putrified.

You will become me –
bone,
naught but bone,
the vital bone
that is
within you,
where I live,
dwell,
abide,
am quick
within you.

We
neither in death nor life can be
 disjoint –
you
live
 by
me
 alone.'


*Note*:

*Ankou is the figure of Death in Breton legend. Representations of him can be found as a free-standing statue or sculpted into church walls, a skeleton carrying variously a scythe, a spear or a spade and sometimes with the motto, 'I kill you all'. Some believe that the last person of the year to die in a village becomes the Ankou of the next year. The maker of this poem has, like the three foolish Rioters in Chaucer's Pardoner's Tale, sought him along the northern coast of Brittany, finding him in out-of-the-way places and through unusual circumstances.*

# Benjamin Keatinge

## Passover

The Monastery of St. Panteleimon at Nerezi

'I had no rest in my spirit . . . but taking my leave of them, I went from thence into Macedonia.' *Second Epistle to the Corinthians*, 2:13.

Because my land has water
more than wine
because my griefs were sheltered
from the wind
I made to travel
to the land of honey-blood
with mountains and a desert
and a trine of Gods
a river and a vineyard
and a host of tongues
a people and a highway
and a cusp of pasts.

I climbed Mount Korab in the sun
knelt at Saint Panteleimon
the heresy was to stand still
the trick was to move on.

138

# Spring, Ballintemple

*On the River Slaney at Ballintemple* by Alexander Williams

Round Patrick's Day we'd set off early
through Wicklow on to Ballintemple,
with gorse flowers neaped in every field
and fish we'd hope were running in the pools
to drift beneath a far-off, trefoiled rim.
You would cast out to a distant ledge
while I would cast about upstream:
we never left that reeling river's edge.
An evening sun would settle on the fields
exhaling lassitude along the hazel weirs
and I would saunter down with empty creel
hoping you'd given up and stowed your gear.
But you would urge me on to one last try,
unfurling line, reaching that furthest lie.

# Alison Brackenbury

## My grandparents' speech

(after a black and white photograph)

Low sounds between words
laughs caught in throat, how
calls bubbled from birds,
their boiling sheets
her gold pie-glaze
his home-dug cabbage
stutter of days
hills' old light, new herds,
silt of leaves under feet
the place between words
we murmur, we meet.

# Judith Shalan

## Light moves

*Inspired by a painting by John Hacker*

Draw me into the dark with you.
Take me deep into your woods and
show me the solid shadows
before they start to smudge and flicker.

Is this the beginning, or is it the end?
It is both, you say.
Light comes of dark and dark of light,
Yin and Yang's slow quickenings turning the day.

They move your brush.
They move my eyes
till I can see those will o' the wisp flicks of light
glancing upwards, then across.

Tiny brushstrokes of fleeting moments
gathering energy, until a glow of white pushes through.
A perfect poise and balance.
Before the letting go.

# Ruth O'Callaghan

## Rohingya

Art Inspiration: *Banishment:* Snezana Pantelic

Let's look at it this way. Exile on an isle
on the edge of action and desire, a smooth
face mirrored in the lake's smooth water,

allows no far away thunder or fractious sea
to break a vow but undertakes to resign
family and friends for a nation, for the world's

service, BBC. Though we know a wise woman
does not carry a flaming torch in a strong wind
we also know that solitude may whisper one

sacrifice is sufficient and silence may mask
many ambitions – the way a negative exposed
to a window's light is distorted when removed.

# Shanta Acharya

## Of Gods and Goddesses

*Based on a tour of an open market in India where shop owners tend to hang
calendars with alluring images of gods and goddesses resembling local film stars.*

The scent of musk melons in the marketplace –
bouncing arcs of desire behind bodices,

luscious the sway of hips of heavenly creatures
with the look of flowers upon their faces.

Irresistible the rush of hormones, pheromones
when the body acquires a mind of its own.

Thrown into a state of confusion, a young man
possessed by an irrepressible hunger bends forward,

legs crossing and re-crossing, half-kneeling
to redeem himself, smelling the lemons stacked

serendipitously on shelves, providing the cover
he needed. Reviving from his fainting spell,

the world in his hands, defying gravity, he
levitates in the heady aura of melons and lemons.

# Damian Walford Davies

## Figure

I'd finished off a chapel
for the Weston Methodists,

ragging them with hints of Hawksmoor
and some wanton puns on Wren.

From my bay, I watched St Mary Street
reviving after rain. Woken by the sun,

O'Driscoll shifted in his oilskin
at the cab-stand; his bowler

held the morning's downpour
as a halo in its rim. I rapped the pane;

he raised his face; the bright ring
sluiced off in a flashing plait.

At the drafting board,
I sketched a figure for a fountain –

water jetting up around her, copper-
cast, mid-jeté, bleeding verdigris.


## Recipe

Spring's promised even to the saltings,
where the coal-dust tide lugs in

to melt the ice-crust in the courses,
then to freeze again. O'Driscoll showed me

samphire, sleeping in its woody stems.
His dead boy foraged with him

for the bright green shoots.
Good to munch on, boiled and slick

with butter come July, he said, or thick
with scallions in a salty champ.

I could taste it in his eyes. Behind him
at the dockside staithes, men sprang

on trucks like bantam devils in a Doom.
*Jim,* I said; *come now, don't cry –*

my awkward naming given music
by the sounding of a two-tone channel buoy.


# Gifts

Some days my mermaid fountain
in Atlantic Square unsettles me –

how her tapered skirt of fishscales
cedes to ruffled bellyskin, how I made her

spew those streams of sloggering
dock water over her own face

until, in last month's northerlies,
she blurred inside chrysalis of ice.

We walk together now, each evening,
in the holm oak avenue behind the house

where the thaw's allowed the jays
to rootle for last autumn's acorns,

cached in pits. As we pass,
they bicker in the branches, flares

of pink and black-barred turquoise
sending showers down like little pentecosts.

# Will Stone

## Goya

By the end he was deaf
but he still heard
the laughter of the insane,
a single claw against the pane
and the scrape of nails
around the asylum wall.
He watched the old witch
bite down on a babe's downy thigh
and saw rough peasants cross the sky
figures falling half-naked
in dispute, in embrace.

Each page, a pale craft gradually passed
through his narrow canal of ink.

Everything turned him upside down
but only insight fell out.
He moved away from men,
forced a passage, his dark prow
broke the ice into bright backgrounds
on which the lonely were placed.
Goya, he forced back the eyelid
of the unseeing, then got out
before it closed again for good.

# Last Rose

After a photograph by Josef Sudek

Bloom born cold
sad as a litter-less pig's eye,
last makeshift raft of colour
adrift on the dark tarn of ivy.
Still life of autumn the scouts
of the first frosts condemned,
casually daubed with a cross.
But elsewhere light is gaining,
sun and birdsong frolic
like oblivious infants, shadows
lay like the weary Antwerp tiger
by the plunge pool, he who succumbed
and was winched out in light rain
above the bristling copse of watchers.
Hawkers of new dawns, humankind
with this retinue of signaling centuries,
kneel and place your old new stone
upon the slow built cairn of history.
Last rose beneath ice where they crowd,
this generation, waiting to enter
the territory of desolation.

# CHOSEN BROADSHEET POETS

## Laura Potts is twenty-two years old and lives in West Yorkshire.
Twice-recipient of the Foyle Young Poets Award, her work has appeared in
*Agenda, Prole* and *Poetry Salzburg Review*. Having worked at The Dylan
Thomas Birthplace in Swansea, Laura was last year listed in The Oxford
Brookes International Poetry Prize and nominated for a Pushcart Prize.
She also became one of The Poetry Business' New Poets and a BBC New
Voice for 2017. Laura's first BBC radio drama aired at Christmas, and she
received a commendation from The Poetry Society in 2018.

## Chatterley

Darling. Your name sleeps hard on my lips. Kiss.
I weep and feel devious, heave my heavy loins
to the window, and wonder at you wondering
at me. Rain. Flesh. Slow thighs and

                    eyes
bright, shut. Put out the candle. Let me tongue
my words through your ear, run through you,
make you mine, the blood in your veins. And
rain on the window like a

                  symphony.
The straw we lay on remembers me: it is shaped
like my body. I tap out your heartbeat on your spine:
*Dum-dum. Dumdum.* See the gold around your ribcage,
the silver of your lung. Now listen to mine.

                     Done.
In the corner, you pull on your shirt. The hurt
of your heart swells in the firelight, spills into the air
between us. Two childhoods glare at each other
across the room. No words. Locked throats.

I feel ten years from you.

Hand me my coat.

# Lady of the Garden

It is the first snow of the year.

In the falling cloak of a coal-cold night and the light
which breathes its last, here with the blood-bright
eyes of stars through dockland fog and foreland far,
our sleeping town remembers you. Ah, spark

and girl of lavender, back-lit in the bygone spring
forever green-of-grape and gone, the wind is bringing
winter on and swings a mist of you towards the gallows
where I am: long the light in which you stand, and oh

the always-infant eyes that sang when shorebirds banked
the garden leaving for another land. And in the blackcurrant
dusk of a fireside lamp is Mam and we, a decade apart, sat
one to each knee. There are more years between us than that.

See, with the fist of the wind came he in a burst of night,
that darkest branch of our ancestry, rising by the candlelight
with looming beaches in his eyes: Death in fighter's finery,
his fatherlight dimmed dull. That bloat upon his skull, berry-

burst and bullet-full, forever thunder-shook the blood
and up-and-swung away the sleeping bud of you, and crooked
the cradle where you stood. Then, oh, the last and lost of love:
he stopped your choral-church of throat. And that was that.

Dawn cracked. Last, a man in a big black hat took you off.
But I still see you, years away, staring past the snowdrops.

# The Body Broken

Mass and Sunday mourning pass the chancel black
and chalice-back of I, spire-spined and last to part
my plumping bud to take the nocturne wine. Mine

the softly hills, mine the spill and steeple-swing
of fruiting breasts and bells, yes. We break the bread
and bless. Lady in the lancet holds the apple mocking red.

Dappled chant and dark, ahead the blood-bright night
and first-light glass of gasping Eve, winter's heave
hangs always here with heads that bow before the vow

to never grieve the leaving eyes of youth. Truth
is lost and winterworn. Borne away on snarling winds,
the greening drop of spring falls from my hair. The cleric's

cloak is a darkly thing. My deeper, deeper throat
receives the gloaming sermon there, heir of the berry
dreamt to burst in his hand. Damn the vestal

up-and-swung of lust that Woman loved, budblood
and the Garden singing skin and pink bouquets, but
turn the tongue beyond the Book and in the darkest

places hold the harvest fruit and look above and long
to lasting-touch the apple that is loathed so much.
Such is Sunday mass and curse of we, the curled

Madonnas kneeling with a screaming in our skirts.
The weakly bread we break and nurse. And vow and
kneel and slaughter one more godless book of verse.

Elizabeth Ridout, 29, a writer of fiction and poetry, is from Yorkshire, currently based in Kent. Her work addresses spiritual experiences in the modern world, feminism, and identity. She is currently working on *Bleach*, her first collection for publication, and her first novel, *A Copper Bath of Beetles*.

## Ariadne

Everyone's always agreed
I've got great legs,
So I suppose it's not unreasonable
To give me a few more
(Even if they are a bit hairier).
But seriously,
That girl has always had it in for me.
Insecure, I suppose -
Some people just can't cope with competition.
It's natural talent,
I can't fight that.
Other women always have been jealous of me:
Great skin, natural talents, pretty eyes,
(So it was really thick of her
To give me six of them).
If she can't handle a bit of healthy rivalry
Then that's her problem.
So petty!
I'm just a creative person,
I'm well known for it,
I've just diversified now –
Getting into decorating nooks, crannies,
Those bits behind the bathroom sink.
I'm infamous now
(Especially amongst the insect community).
It just goes to show
Pride doesn't have to come before a fall,
I bungee-snap back
On my unbreakable spirit
And my satin suspender strings.

# A photograph of my mother, 18, in August 1977

You began me with a cry to a God
Who wasn't listening.
I flew in like those forty year old dandelion clocks at your feet
To a Madonna in platforms and suede.

My fingertips sing out for yours.
I saw you through a rose quartz
At first
Now you are a yellowing snapshot

Standing at the end of a garden path.
Mouth mimicking the endless O of the lens
In a permanently air-borne kiss
That flutters through decades.

Eyes squeezed joyfully
Against the flare of flash and flame of roses –
You know nothing
And are revelling in it.

Were you waiting for me?

Holding your hands up against the camera's approving nod
Like a mask it is a pleasure to wear,
Finger faced.
I am a glint in the camera's lens

Before I grabbed you round the middle
And you belonged to me.

# The Taxidermist

Shaved-leg prickle,
Palely veined as a pebble,

Taupe as a split sausage –
Your paw-pink rawness,

Peeled like an eyeball
For a blindfolded Halloween party game.

An indecency of stitching
Could frame you –

Needle you into place,
Like a saddle for a penny farthing,

Padding for a fainting couch,
Or stuffing for a brothel bench.

Lie still, this will hurt –

I can mount you,
Mahogany or rosewood?

I can put you in a bell jar
For a literary flourish
And to keep away the fleas;

Dress you up in a voodoo jazz cat's
Shrunken head's top hat
Or the bonnet of a mouse on the Havisham cake, perhaps

The apron of a rat from the Lovetts' kitchen.
I have Growltiger's eyepatch
And Algernon's flowers.

The profane and the sacred,
The kitsch and the slimy

Will allow you
To be eaten by moths instead of by worms
In the comfort of your own living room.

# Briony Collins

Briony Collins is a 22-year-old Literature student at Bangor University. She has just completed her first year. She has been writing poetry for many years, but it has recently focused on issues with civil rights as this has been the subject she has been writing about for the past two years in her novel, *Raise Them Up*. She has been tutored by Carol Ann Duffy, Gillian Clarke, Paul Henry, and Catherine Fisher on courses at Ty Newydd. She won the 2016 Exeter Novel Prize.She was longlisted for the 2016 National Poetry Competition with her poem 'Divorce.' This year she is a recipient of a Literature Wales bursary.

## Liberty

Violin string mark
mayflower fingers
while mine blister.
We smile together
and smoke our pipes
down to embers.
Toes tap the same
southern rhythm:
them, in the stables,
me, outside with the
horses, whistling
intimations of liberty.

**Jack Priestnall** is a creative writing undergrad in his early twenties at Bangor University, Wales.

## Aboudia's Talking Heads

The streets of this place are hectic and dynamic,
struggling with chaos.

All the children stand waiting,
watching and staring at me.

Why do they stare, have they never seen
a man as bland as me in blue Africa?

Face simple lined with no etching scars, White not Black.
No mixing colours of my own. No grey areas.

I think that's why they stare.


**Helen Rear** is a 21-year-old English Literature and Creative Writing student at Bangor University. She is a three-time consecutive winner of National Novel Writing Month and is currently working on her debut poetry collection. When not writing, Helen runs a Youtube channel which focuses on reviewing books of various genres.

## Jaws

Picasso's shark lurks
in stark blueprints.
his aggravated eye quivers
on the shelf.

pink-tinged jaws glitter
while kiwi slices dribble toxic juices
over chalked walls,
white smears
on rusted paraphernalia.

the whole shack shudders,
lungs lingering
on the last breath.

# NOTES FOR BROADSHEET POETS
In conversation with Martyn Crucefix

**P McC**: Although your sequence, *A Hatfield Mass* (Worple Press, 2014), is the length of a pamphlet, it is a work of major poetic and philosophical significance. Who would you say were your main influences here?

**MC**: In proper ekphrastic fashion, I'd have to say the main influence on the poems was Henry Moore's art itself. With the exception of the little coda of lyrics (a loose translation of a German text), I wanted the physical presence of the sculptures and their placement in the summer garden landscape of Hatfield House to constitute the bulk of, and to flow through, each poem. So the substance of the sequence is summed up in its subtitle: 'voice and shape in an English landscape'. Beyond that, I remember I'd been reading Yves Bonnefoy's work, particularly the poem 'De Vente et de Fumée' in which he describes beauty as a 'regretting' and the work of art as 'gathering up / By the handful nothing but absent water' (tr. John Naughton). Moore's art – full of its sensuous curves and holes, many pieces not figurative yet suggestive of figures – reminded me of Bonnefoy's idea that a good poem is an ever-failing, but never-ceasing, effort to capture that fluidity and unity of being which he calls 'presence'.

**P McC**: Rilke, too, whose *Duino Elegies* (Enitharmon, 2006) and *Sonnets to Orpheus* (Enitharmon, 2012) you translated to great acclaim, seems not far away in the tone and range of breadth here.

**MC**: I spent about fifteen years working on Rilke's two great sequences of poems, so I suspect his influence is never far from my everyday conversation let alone anything I have written ever since! But I'm also a great believer that subjects choose poets as much as the other way around, so the time I devoted to Rilke was evidence that his ideas rhymed with something already laid up in me, however inchoately. I was so impressed with your poem 'Word-Bells' in *Rodin's Shadow* in which Clara Westhoff addresses Rilke's 'preference to become // invisible'. In the Orpheus sonnets he declares, 'Travel always towards transformation' and it is a challenging of the boundaries of the self that he has in mind there. I always see those boundaries as smouldering, smoking – at certain moments – becoming less-defined, absorbing elements of what lies beyond and, with the force of a revelation, I saw something of that in Moore's sun-lit, curving, gaping and penetrated shapes.

**P McC**: I also, because of the title, couldn't help but think of David Jones' unfinished *Kensington Mass* published by Agenda Editions. Was this in the back of your mind?

**MC**: I'm afraid I don't know it – but I will now look it up!

**P McC**: And while we are talking about the Mass, sub-titles to your poems follow the strict pattern of the Catholic Mass, with the kyrie, gloria, credo, sanctus, benedictus, agnus dei – and then the coda. Can you explain how, exactly, your actual poems link to the different parts of the Mass?

**MC**: At a certain stage, I had a lot of the text written but was struggling to find an ordering principle for it – I like sequences of poems to have an architecture of some kind. It was clear early on that there was no real narrative thread to the ekphrastic writing, though there were autobiographical fragments that cropped up in several places, memories and occasions which had spontaneously – but not irrelevantly – been spun off from writing about Moore's art. One evening at the Barbican, I was following the sequence of the Mass in the programme notes and began to think this might be an answer. Could I remove God from the equation but still retain the outline of a cry for mercy, a poem of praise, of belief, of worship (in this case mistakenly) and finally of the lamb/child. The Coda is a very loose and (again) de-deified version of an anonymous text used by Bach in his cantata 'Iche habe genug'.

**P McC**: Going back to influences or resonances, some of your thinking here seems to tally with T S Eliot in his *Four Quartets* particularly. Like the latter, are you attempting to 'say the unsayable'?

**MC**: If that doesn't sound too pretentious – I hope so. The *Quartets* is so monumental and abstract that I find it hard to like as a whole. I do prefer the earlier Eliot. But the lines in 'Little Gidding' about not ceasing 'from exploration' always make my hair stand on end (in a good way) and this is indeed what the Bach-sourced *nunc dimittis* poems of my Coda are supposed to enact – not so much Simeon's traditional death and ascent to Heaven but the perceiving self's death and renewal as part of an on-going process of what Keats called 'Soul-making': my 'agnus dei' poem talks of a process of becoming: 'if not more beautiful we grow more rich'.

**P McC**: There I would disagree with you – *The Four Quartets* is, to me, the summation of Eliot's work. But, as ekphrastic poetry, how did you set about writing this sequence, Martyn? Did you sit there with Henry Moore's sculptures when they were exhibited in the grounds of Hatfield House, Hertfordshire, in 2011?

MC: In a word, yes. I visited the exhibition on a very crowded Sunday with others and enjoyed it in a rather superficial way – the sunshine, bird-song, the light gleaming on the bronze and marble forms, a cup of tea in the café. But that evening I couldn't get the images out of my mind and I went back, alone, on the much quieter following day. I stood and sat before a number of the pieces and simple wrote rapidly into a notebook. Little of what I have said in this interview about Bonnefoy, Rilke or other contributaries was consciously in my mind at the time, but I felt I could trust the moment enough because I knew it was all being fuelled by a certain emotional state. I even felt I could take on trust the scraps of autobiography that forced their way in.

P McC: I really like the way the sculptures are solidly there, sensuous as the language you weave around them which progresses at a very steady rhythm, like a basso continuo.

MC: I'm really happy if there is a musical quality about the language and the structure of the whole thing. I wanted the poems to lift off from the ground more ambitiously than I often manage to achieve and the abstraction of music seemed a good model to follow though I hope the whole remains rooted in the wonderful, tactile, 'thinginess' of Moore's art (you always feel propelled to move forward to touch them) as well as the sensuous images of the garden and the natural world.

P McC: Solipsism is a big concern of yours and how to escape it – as you explain in your end-note. It appears that you take the act of making love with another person/body a way out of the prison of the self.

MC: Admittedly, not a very original thought – and often an idealised view of the act or an elevating of it into metaphor. But the sheer sexiness of Moore's figures – all the pieces I ended up writing about were female figures, one or two with young children – contributed to this theme certainly. Early in the sequence there is a young man, wholly preoccupied with himself; there are unsatisfactory moments of physical love-making; there are other moments in which the couple can hardly tell themselves apart; there are others where mother or father and child achieve a remarkable closeness.

P McC: The sculptures seem to allow you to insert private, intimate experiences into the poems, along with lyrical images, in order to demonstrate how we can progress to include the whole world, shedding, by a process of little deaths, old selves on the way to proper attentiveness and plenitude.

MC: Can I not reply to this except to say that what you say is precisely what I had hoped to convey?

P McC: You could say that the sculpted forms are totally solipsistic in a symbolic way, locked up as they are inside the stone or whatever it is they are composed of. Yet your interpretation in the poems frees them from this, giving them an outer objective meaning. I noticed in an early poem, the persona (you?) wants to 'lick' the sculpture:

> ...slicing through the body my hands go
> burrow and under and between the air

Was this a deliberate parallel to what, we, as humans, should be striving for?

MC: I'm remembering the eroticism of John Donne in those lines: 'Licence my roving hands, and let them go, / Before, behind, between, above, below' ('To His Mistress Going to Bed'). In fact, I think the *absence* of anything solipsistic in most of these forms by Henry Moore is what excited me in the first place. Without realistically representing the human form, he manages to put the human body into a relationship with its surroundings, to achieve a sort of porousness, the inner and outer bleeding and blurring into one another. This is harder to experience in a museum or gallery space – but set in the Hatfield House grounds this is what struck me so powerfully. In this sense, the ekphrastic inspiration really did create the poetry and, in another time or place, nothing might ever have come from it. The sense of freedom in image and verse forms is also attributable to Moore's sculptures. As I've implied already, the fixed edges of the self are already wobbling in his work and there is an invitation to observers to go up and touch – perhaps to lick! – and that invitation seemed to me to extend even to the surrounding landscape too: come and be one, at least for a brief instant!

*

MC: Your *Rodin's Shadow* is such an ambitious project, I wondered, of course, what the origins of it were – was it in the fascinating biographies, the art of Rodin, the art of Camille Claudel or Gwen John, or of more personal origin?

**P McC**: Well, when I lived in Paris for four years many years ago, I used to go and sit in the garden of the Musée Rodin, close to *The Thinker*. Not many people seemed to know about the Musée Rodin then, so it was my secret little haven. I didn't know about his mistresses in those days and I can't quite recall what got me fascinated with Camille Claudel. I wrote a few poems in her voice, having read about her harrowing life and deliberately left Rodin out, as it seemed she had been given a very raw deal by him. However, what got me going in greater earnest was a second hand book in French sent to me from Westport, Co Mayo by my great Irish friend who found it in an open-air bookstall. As I read through, I found some lines in French from a letter she had written to Rodin that I had actually written in English in a poem, the exact words: 'I am sleeping completely naked/ in make-belief that you are here'. This gave me the shivers down my spine as I felt somehow she had entered into me psychically and I was called upon to write through her. This I did, some poems being more definitely ekphrastic, and sub-headed by the particular name of the sculpture that inspired the poem and which I studied in the little room dedicated to her work in the Musée Rodin – such a small space, even though Rodin had told her that she was more talented than him.

A gifted young actress whom I had taught then performed some of them with me, in echoing and overlapping voices, in front of the actual sculpture, Rodin's *The Kiss*, which was lent to Lewes Town Hall at the time.

The poems on Gwen John, Rose Beuret and Clara Westhoff I didn't write until quite a few years later when my energy had returned and I felt I could tackle them.

Some of the poems are fuelled by my own personal experiences so that I could feel what they felt, and get inside their skin the way a translator ideally wants to do with the poet he/she is translating. I also tried to get inside their skins the way an actor does with the character he/she is portraying. A few of the poems were old ones in different shapes that I re-wrote until they fitted in.

**MC**: However it began, there is so much research evident in the sequence, how did you manage to maintain the balance so well between that book-learning side and the more creative, empathetic side of writing poems about these women?

**P McC**: I don't really know. All I can say is that I experienced the poems as I was writing them and felt the emotion being conveyed, tinged, often but by no means always, with what I have experienced in my life, so that they didn't come from without but were somehow intrinsic. I suppose with, say, for Camille Claudel whom I concentrated on in the first lot of poems, I immersed myself in her life (from books) and I wasn't conscious of having to wed the book-learning side with the more creative side of writing the poem. I deliberately didn't let myself watch the film on her, because I didn't want to be swayed by any images or scenes that the film-maker might impose on me, as these might have swayed me and in a way interfered with all that was in my head, and imagination.

MC: How far did you foresee, or come to see, the book as a chance to put the four women's side of the story, a perspective perhaps too little told in conventional art history?

P McC: As I say, it all happened kind of organically, over quite a few years, with the break in between. When I did get back to the poems and took on the three other women, Gwen John, Rose Beuret and Rilke's wife, Clara Westhoff who was an accomplished yet hardly recognised sculptor in her own right, I felt it was important to continue (from the initial Camille Claudel poems) to get inside the minds and lives of these women who had, as far as I knew, been mostly obscured from history. My indignation at the way they had been treated was the engine behind the poems. There is a strange parallel between Camille and Gwen John in that they were both similarly obsessed with Rodin who of course led them on with his undoubted magnetism. I suppose I can be obsessive, too, so I understood where they were coming from. I did want to put Rodin in his place, via his absence in my pages, as he was a bit of a bastard with these women, and, of course, he was so exalted world-wide. When you think of it, mainly because of him, Camille Claudel ended up spending more than the last thirty years of her life in an asylum where she refused ever to sculpt again (apart from a few crude pencil-drawn caricatures of Rodin on all fours as a beast), and she was equally mistreated by her brother, Paul Claudel the playwright, as well as by her very own mother. I make out in my book that she was never really insane at all, which I think is true. The same with Gwen John: she swapped her passion for Rodin for a passion for God and then ended up, it seems, taking her own life and dying unknown in a side-street of Dieppe. To give a voice to Klara, the wife of Rilke, Rodin's secretary for a while, I steeped myself in my old battered copies of Rilke's letters that I had absorbed years ago, and, again, with some sort of annoyance, wanted to give her a voice so that she wasn't just a kind of mirror image for Rilke, a backdrop, someone always there, neglected and long-suffering – similar to the illiterate Rose Beuret whom Rodin married in his youth and weirdly remained with her, despite his many dalliances, all their joint life.

**MC**: You preface the whole book with an image of Penelope as almost patron-saint of these women who have been variously 'lost / to masters of stone and script'. Do the images of stitching and threads, patterns and themes, suggest something of the process of the writing about their different lives?

**P McC**: Exactly that, Martyn. I was aware in the writing – or stitching – of related themes and patterns of images that evolve, criss-cross and connect throughout.

**MC**: The closing lines of the whole book, on Camille Claudel's funeral, express extraordinary anger: she's 'sealed in the earth by a line / that stretched into a tight, sadistic, spade-edged grin'. Can you say something about anger as a motivating force in the writing?

**P McC**: Yes, and I think I just touched on this earlier. I did feel anger, coupled with a huge sense of injustice, about the way all four women were mistreated and neglected. The anger was a subliminal driving force, if you like, but once distilled, anger becomes more objectified, and this made my compassion all the greater for the women. They needed standing up for.

Also, of course, in the actual poems, some of the women express their own justifiable raw anger: Camille against Rodin, Gwen, too, against Rodin, Rose against Camille and Rodin, and Klara just a little against Rilke with all his philanderings.

**MC**: You speak eloquently for the women and their common suffering and yet, in a poem like 'Mistress of Rags', Rose Beuret addresses Camille with a mixture of envy and eventual triumph. How does the sequence deal with the differences between the women as well as what they shared?

**P McC**: I tried to work out each separate character and how each would react when in the presence of the other one. Camille and Gwen were more similar in their over-riding obsessions with Rodin (cultivated by the latter) – and I even gave them a duet called 'Cats Chorus', whereas poor, long-suffering Rose, the 'Mistress of Rags', never had a chance to have either a voice or an art form in which to express herself. She was reduced to wrapping his sculptures in rags until the end of her life with the mechanical rhythm of: 'Slip slap slop slip./ Rags in a bucket I squeeze and dip.'

And she did, definitely, suffer over Rodin's mistresses, when she was treated like dirt and as his maid. This is why, in the poem you mention, I was delighted that she could have her moment of triumph over Camille. I did, too, to keep her realistic, try to give her an uneducated voice, different in tone from the others. For example, I gave her quite a lot of rhyming couplets and monosyllabic words, yet a dignity in her voice and a gift at times of irony. As for Rilke's wife, I let her show her eternal dedication to her husband, as well as her analysis of him, along with her mocking tone when she takes pleasure in citing in satirical rhyming couplets the names of all his mistresses.

Because Gwen John wrote over two thousand letters in two years to Rodin, I focus on a few letters from her (which link back to the letters Camille sent Rodin from two different chateaux where she stayed alone, in one recovering from a possible abortion), instead of ekphrastic poems inspired by her paintings.

**MC**: Rose Beuret emerges out of the story as something of a survivor – she actually married Rodin at a very late stage. You describe her as 'semi-literate' and I wondered what challenges portraying her presented to you as a poet?

**P McC**: As I have already mentioned, I was aware of having to alter the tone in her voice to something more colloquial. Various devices helped me, such as repetition, monosyllabic rhyme, sometimes couplets, sometimes deliberately jarring lack of rhyme. However, I wasn't really aware of these devices when I wrote the poems. I left her with snippets in French too, and surrounded her by animals and a coachman in the poem with its ironic title 'Duchesse' – to earth her. She might have been semi-literate but she was also insightful. She is further praised by a poem in Gwen John's voice. Here Gwen imagines the two of them being friends, and she, Gwen, learning how to sew from Rose, and she pictures how they could have both catwalked 'in the Hotel Bîron – up, down,// over the mosaic of his own black stones'.

**MC**: Perhaps inevitably, I'm fascinated by the Rodin-shaped hole – his striking absence – in the sequence. I'm presuming that was a crucial, deliberate and early decision?

**P McC**: It was as you say: just that, fired by indignation on my part. For example, in the poem, 'Camille's bust of Rodin', bronze 1888, I show how Rodin 'hoodwinked/ experts it was a self-portrait on his plinth'. I ask you: stealing from the woman artist just as Scott Fitzgerald stole the best bits from his wife Zelda's letters and diaries, and from the manuscript of her one and only novel *Save me the Waltz*. Again, in the second part of the three-part poem 'Cet homme couvert de femmes' (Rose's ironic title for Rodin), entitled 'Portrait de Madame Rodin, Mère, circa 1870', I show, in Rose's voice, her indignation at Rodin claiming that the bust of herself as a lovely young girl was that of Rodin's mother. Such injustice, not allowing Rose to be immortalized in her youth as a beauty and not as 'poor old Rose' as she came to be called.

**MC**: Given my interest in Rilke – who worked as Rodin's secretary for a while in Paris – I felt that the poet was more present in a number of the poems than Rodin himself was at any point. I take it they are 'the masters of stone and script'. Are they condemned alike in your view?

**P McC**: Rodin is condemned, but of course one has to respect his work. And, apparently, if I am to be kind, he never got over the loss of a sister when he was young and someone told me this marked him – and was ironically perhaps why he stuck to Rose and ultimately rejected Camille, even though he said he would marry her.

Rilke is different. Like you, I am very attached personally to Rilke, especially to his *Duino Elegies*. I got close to him in his letters and his novel about his nervous breakdown in Paris – a long time ago. Klara, in my sequence, gently mocks him for all his ladies, but is longsuffering in a different way to Rose, and rather than resenting him, she demonstrates her admiration for him and her attunement with him. Perhaps I was biased.

**MC**: More broadly, how far should we condemn such politically incorrect (male) artists – Picasso springs to mind – or are they permitted some redemption because of the art they produced? This seems a very topical issue.

**P McC**: I suppose their art works exist despite the details of their makers' lives. So their art has to be judged without them. Think of Thomas Hardy's wonderfully moving 1912-13 poems, elegies you would take to your grave with you, so haunting and beautifully crafted and it doesn't matter that he most likely wrote them out of guilt as he hated his wife Emma when she was alive; wouldn't go anywhere with her and even made out she was mad. The poems have their own life, just as the art works do – as you show so well in your Henry Moore sequence.

**MC**: One of the most explicitly ekphrastic poems is 'Your Hand', alluding to sculptures by both Rodin and Camille Claudel. Can you say something about that poem?

**P McC**: Yes. I found it interesting that both had independently sculpted hands. Rodin called his 'La Cathédrale', stone, 1908, delineating his interest and expertise in cathedrals and in his sculpting the architecture of a human hand into a cathedral, in a kind of metaphor; hers was merely 'La Main', bronze vers 1885. In this poem I let Camille show her desire for Rodin as a protector, enrapturer, reassurer, lover. The first line of every first stanza is the same, showing her insistent desire, and the last two lines of each of the four five-lined verses ends in a rhyming couplet, symbolizing her desire for the two of them to rhyme together, as one.

**MC**: You open the book with a cast list and several of the poems suggest you composed them as speeches, almost dialogues, and others gesture towards settings and stage directions. Were you ever tempted to adopt a more dramatic form?

**P McC**: Because many of the poems are dramatic monologues and there is a narrative (no matter how I have jumbled up sequences of events, and drawn some of the characters together so that they interact) – yes I envisaged the whole sequence as a drama that could well be acted out on a stage, given more stage directions and some props, also music at times beneath the words, at times between poems or different sections e.g. of Debussy, and Saint-Saëns, also waltzes – plus Gregorian chant and church bells. This would be the ideal reading for the book: with contrasting voices, echoing and overlapping at times, chorusing too as they spark off each other and so on. In fact, I have already mentioned I and a friend produced parts of the book in dramatic form (e.g. letting Camille and Gwen share a few poems such as 'The Waltz' because symbolically they were similar in their obsessions). We also performed a more major part of the sequence when the book was finished, again in front of Rodin's 'The Kiss' in The Turner Gallery in Margate. Here we had all the personages from the sequence, including Debussy who is the only man to be allowed a small voice in the book (Camille had a brief affair with him when trying to get over Rodin at one point). Touchingly, Debussy kept for the rest of his life Camille's sculpture of 'The Waltz' on the lid of his piano.

**MC**: Through the love, grief, anger and madness you maintain a remarkable sense of poetic form or forms. Was that important to you?

**P McC**: Very important – for variety, for changes in tone and emotion. Some of the different rhyming forms and rhythms, the different kinds of repetition, and indeed deliberate lack of rhyme in places just happened in the writing of them.

*

165

And now, Martyn, let's talk more about your *Hatfield Mass*. Your poems are about shifts, changes and passing – yet the sculptures, even with their 'flex and curve', are basically immobile, fixed. Can you comment on this?

**MC**: The genius of Moore was to make these hefty forms yet to give them a sense of movement. One of the pieces I wrote about is a female figure laid back on her elbows but with her head turned as if listening momentarily to something behind her. This seemed to me a wonderful image of the kind of heightened perception that can occasionally occur. In such a moment we shuck off the rigidity of our more everyday perception – the utilitarian assumptions that self and other are separate – to see the essential interconnectedness that is the truth in epistemological, interpersonal, political and, of course, ecological terms. Moore's shapes allowed me to explore such abstract issues in tangible forms. The poems are also obsessed with change and things passing because we cannot maintain such a level of freshness of perception for very long. There is something in our make-up, perhaps something to do with a basic survival instinct, that drives us to firm up, solidify, indeed petrify – turn to stone – such fluid perceptions. This is Bonnefoy's insight and there is a pleasure in the irony that it took marble and bronze figures in a landscape to produce poems that explore that petrification process.

**P McC**: How deliberate was it that, like me with Rodin, you kept Henry Moore out of your poems?

**MC**: I never wanted there to be a biographical element to the poems – so very different to your own original impulse with *Rodin's Shadow*. The titles we each chose for the sequences written are very revealing, aren't they? I had in mind delicate, lyrical poems tracing elements and shifts in perception which – I hoped – might amount to a sort of spiritual exploration of the negotiations that continual occur between inner and outer. As we've discussed, your Rodin is astonishingly absent from most of the sequence, yet present as a shadow cast over the lives of those around him.

**P McC**: Yes, well I chose the biographical element as a way of getting into the actual impulses of the works. After all, Camille Claudel's sculptures in particular are inspired almost exclusively by her own personal experiences. I wanted, in a different ekphrastic manner, to get into her mind, how she felt and why, in the making of the sculptures that I focus upon – rather like the way a translator tries to capture the spirit or essence of the poet he/she is translating and comes out with versions of the original, then finds these closer to the foreign poet than any literal translation can be.

Back to you, though. I like the way you imply the sculpted figures have their own kind of speech: 'this encircling arc/ of her cradle-arms/ is more speech than fear' (5 'Mother and Child' – *Benedictus*).

MC: Poetry is the Antaeus art form – it re-grounds us in what is important: love, death, time and language. We are always short-cutting, for utilitarian reasons of survival, the complicated truths of these things. Poetry reminds us of the shifting, fluid complexities at the heart of our lives. Language is the model for this; we are always resorting to cliché when the truth would be better expressed with greater care and by pushing the boundaries of everyday language. As our own body language can be more truthfully revealing than our speech, I thought Moore's figures expressed themselves in a gestural language which challenged the clichés we more often fall back on.

P McC: Beautifully said. And this is connected to the absence of punctuation in the poems, the repetitions, the echoes and refrains?

MC: Absolutely. The progressive removal of punctuation is something that has been happening to my poems over a number of years. It is both a difficulty and a liberation in that it allows ambiguity and fluidity. It allows – I hope – the poem to be more 'of a moment', all its elements held in the reader's mind in a moment rather than in a temporal sequence. This is supposed to more truly represent the unity of 'presence' before it succumbs to divisions of time and grammar. The repetitions, the echoes and refrains in *A Hatfield Mass* are also performing a similar function: using the linear form of language to suggest that experiences are co-present, recurring, fluidly ebbing and flowing in and out of consciousness.

P McC: There's so much I'd like to quote from your sequence. These two particular lines keep coming back to me:

What has shape and expires to shapelessness
To which we give words against all wordlessness

To 'give words against all wordlessness'. Isn't that what all poets endeavour to do?

MC: I like those lines too! What we think we know for sure is always liable to ebb and fade into the truth of the greater whole and the reverse process is that, from our brief sensing of that greater whole, we are always trying to pluck elements from it, to secure them into some sort of stability through

conception which is fundamentally a linguistic process. We name things –
as Adam did – and they shimmy into existence, but poetry always reminds
us of their true impermanence, that we are not separate from them in truth.

**P McC** : In your wonderful end Coda, you invoke Bach's cantata 'Ich habe
genug', the librettist unknown. Was there any reason you expanded your
Mass into musical ekphrasis? The shape of it is so pure and spacious – and
with its refrain, 'Now I have enough', you almost set it to your own music
in your head when reading it...

**MC**: A bit pretentiously I had two models in mind: Shelley's *Prometheus
Unbound* and Goethe's *Faust*. Both pretend to record the songs of
disembodied natural spirits and their implied vital animation of nature
seemed right for my sequence too with its premise that self and other
are really interwoven. The brevity of the Bach libretto pieces appealed –
evoking the swift passage of time – as did that sentiment of 'Now I have
enough'. It expresses not so much a contentment and reaching of stasis
but a readiness to move on, to be prepared for a new re-formulation of our
relationships with the other, whatever they may be.

**P McC**: Interesting, too, as I did the same though differently with *Rodin's
Shadow* by bringing in Debussy, the only man to have a very small voice in
the sequence. But towards the end, I wrote a piece while actually listening
to Debussy, part v of 'Camille on her Deathbed in the Asylum' from the
last section, 'Fag Ends'. I wrote down the images that came to me while
listening to 'La Mer', like a given poem from the music.

**MC**: I did the same, listening over and over to the Bach cantata – a piece
that long before I thought of using it in this way had been a favourite of
mine. As you say, interesting that we both arrived at forms of *musical
ekphrasis*, in your case inspired by Debussy's biographical presence in the
Rodin story, in mine prompted by finding myself arriving at something
closer to a religious sense than I have ever tried to express in poetic form. I
was suddenly aware that, for the first time in my writing career, I wanted to
use the word 'soul' without any irony at all.

**P McC**: That word 'soul', properly defined, is an important one, Martyn,
and one that many are afraid of, or won't even consider.
   Thank you very much, Martyn, for taking part in this conversation.

**MC**: Thank you and thank you *Agenda*.

# John Robert Lee

## My work with Ekphrastic Poetry.

I am not a painter or sculptor, but I have always been interested in art and artists. I am an amateur photographer and have been using camera and film from my school days at St. Mary's College. In recent times I have been using a point and shoot digital camera and now find myself using mainly my phone which has a good camera. As a writer of poetry, prose fiction and non-fiction; as a former theatre actor and director – the compositional and dramatic elements of art, photography and film have been a tremendous guide to me as I compose using the materials of language to shape line, sentence, image, metaphor. I compose to hold, in form, the content of emotion, thought and intuition, and somehow to frame some meaning out of the palette of multi-hued experience.

I don't recall when I first started writing 'ekphrastic' poetry. I don't even remember if I had seen examples and had been moved to try my hand. In fact I only became aware of the term 'ekphrastic' when the Jamaican poet, Kei Miller, seeing my poems on the work of St. Lucian artist Gary Butte, responded, 'oh, ekphrastic poetry.' So, I did not know I was writing ekphrastic poetry until that epiphanic moment!

The images I have been working with include photographs (mine and those of others) and art – classical and contemporary. In public reading of the poems I have also been working with projections of the images and allowing my reading to serve as a sound-track to the pictures.

How do I approach the writing of ekphrastic poetry? Usually I would come across an image I like, or in other cases I would deliberately choose an image or sequence of images, that I want to work with, as with local painters Gary Butte and Shallon Fadlien. Then I begin to look (literally) long and hard at the images. This can happen over a long period of time, usually, though sometimes, it may not be very long. In contemplating, meditating on the images, I am trying to respond intellectually, emotionally, intuitively to them. I don't want to literally describe the image. I want to find what the image says to me. I also want the images to connect with, and pull out of my deepest mind, some parallel thought, image, feeling, intuition.

Then whatever intuitive, emotional or intellectual response that begins to form also begins to find, to seek, the best form of poem that will suit the image: variety of diction, line length, stanza form, rhythmic devices etc, all the usual paraphernalia of poetry.

In a kind of way, my approach is that of those who make ikons: I am referring to the ikon-making tradition of the Eastern Orthodox Christian traditions. The poem itself is becoming an ikon, whose compositional material is not dyes and canvas or wood, but language. (Eddie Baugh, the Jamaican poet and critic, has written that 'all literature is ultimately about language.') And I raise the making of ikons, since my approach to writing ekphrastic poetry follows a kind of similar approach: personal preparation, entering a space of quiet contemplation, finding a resting point between my consciousness and the image that allows the exposition, the exploration, the responding to take shape.

I discovered some time ago that the process of making ikons is actually called 'writing the ikon.' (According to the Orthodox, ikons are not to be worshipped, but are an aid to contemplation of divinity, Christ, the saints.) What a metaphor for writers and in a special way for one who regards poems themselves as ikons. Here is a poem I wrote out of that learning called 'Writing the ikon'.

# Writing the ikon

You must now enter the silence alone and listen. Wait.
Wait for the translation of the first line. Write.
Write with your fingers searching the pigments on the palate
for the essential shading of the right
image. The medium frames the sacred intercession.
To give face, posture and voice to the holy is no trite
matter. And where humility unveils some gracious incarnation,
offer first this blessed sacrament to the King of saints.

In the case of this poem, it was not initially ekphrastic since the image was not the inspiration of the poem (which is part of a cycle called 'Canticles'). I later added the image (my photograph of a carving I own) as an illustration. The poem, however, while it seeks to describe the process of artistic and poetry creation, does illustrate to some extent, my approach to writing ekphastic poems. So it could be called an ekphrastic poem with the poem coming first and the art fitting it.

# Biographies

**Shanta Acharya** was born and educated in Cuttack, India. She won a scholarship to Oxford, and was among the first batch of women admitted to Worcester College. A recipient of the Violet Vaughan Morgan Fellowship, she was awarded the Doctor of Philosophy for her work on Ralph Waldo Emerson. She was a Visiting Scholar in the Department of English and American Literature and Languages at Harvard University before joining Morgan Stanley, an American investment bank, in London. She worked in the asset management industry and has written extensively on the subject. The author of eleven books, her publications range from poetry, literary criticism and fiction to finance. Her latest book is *Imagine: New and Selected Poems*. Founder of *Poetry in the House*, Shanta hosted a series of monthly poetry readings at Lauderdale House, Highgate, London, from 1996-2015. In addition to her philanthropic activities, she served twice on the board of trustees of the Poetry Society in the UK and served twice on the board of trustees of the Poetry Society in the UK.

**Gary Allen**'s seventeenth collection, *The Glass King*, will be published this Summer by Stairwell Books. Poems widely published in international literary magazines including *Ambit, Agenda, Australian Book Review, London Magazine, The New Statesman, Poetry Review, Stand, The Threepenny Review*.

**William Bedford**'s poetry has appeared in *Agenda, The Dark Horse, The Frogmore Papers, Encounter, The Interpreter's House, The John Clare Society Journal, London Magazine, The Malahat Review, The New Statesman, Poetry Review, Poetry Salzburg Review, The Tablet, Temenos, The Warwick Review, The Washington Times* and many others. Red Squirrel Press published *The Fen Dancing* in March 2014 and *The Bread Horse* in October 2015. He won first prize in the 2014 *London Magazine* International Poetry Competition.

**Alison Brackenbury**'s ninth collection, *Skies*, (Carcanet, 2016), featured on Radio 4 and was one of *The Observer's* Poetry Books of the Year. New poems can be read at her website: www.alisonbrackenbury.co.uk

**Peter Carpenter**'s next collection is due from Two Rivers Press in 2020. A *New and Selected Poems, Just Like That*, was published by Smith/Doorstop. Poems have appeared in many literary journals including the *TLS, Poetry Review, Poetry Ireland Review, Agenda, Snow*, the *Independent* and the *Independent on Sunday*. He is co-director and editor of Worple Press.

**Martin Caseley** has retired from teaching to the obscurity of Norfolk. Recent essays and reviews have appeared in *Agenda, PN Review* and on the *Stride* website. He is working on a sequence of poems on Wymondham Abbey and continuing to write further essays.

**David Cooke** won a Gregory Award in 1977. Since then his work has appeared in many journals in the UK, Ireland and beyond: *Agenda, Ambit, The Cortland Review, The Interpreter's House, The Irish Times, The London Magazine, Magma, The Manhattan Review, The Morning Star, The North, Poetry Ireland Review, Poetry Salzburg Review* and *Stand. After Hours*, his fifth collection, was published in 2017 by Cultured Llama Press. He is the founding editor of *The High Window*.

**D. V. Cooke (David Vincent Cooke)** was born in Cheshire and graduated in English from London University. He worked for a number of years for The Poetry Library in London and has published in numerous poetry magazines including: *Acumen, Babel, Envoi, Frogmore Papers, Orbis, Outposts, Poetry Wales, Stand, Swansea Review, Tandem* and *Agenda*.

**Martyn Crucefix** has published 7 collections of poetry, most recently *The Lovely Disciplines* (Seren, 2017) and *O. at the Edge of the Gorge (Guillemot, 2017)*. His translation of Rilke's *Duino Elegies* (Enitharmon, 2006) was shortlisted for the Popescu Prize for European Poetry Translation and hailed as "unlikely to be bettered for very many years" (Magma). Other translations include Rilke's *The Sonnets to Orpheus* (Enitharmon, 2012) and the *Daodejing* (Enitharmon, 2016).

**Peter Dale** has had many volumes of poetry, and translations published mainly by Agenda Editions, Anvil Press and Carcanet, also a book on dowsing. He lives in Wales and, despite struggles with his health and his bereavement over his life-long wife, he is still writing poetry.

**Damian Walford Davies** is the author of *Suit of Lights* (Seren, 2009), *Witch* (Seren, 2012), *Judas* (Seren, 2015), *Alabaster Girls* (Rack Press, 2015) and the forthcoming ghost story in verse, *Docklands* (Seren). His next collection — *Go, Go, Gino Bartali!* — is a poetic engagement with the great Italian cyclist and two-time Tour de France winner. He is Head of the School of English, Communication and Philosophy at Cardiff University.

**Gerald Dawe**'s most recent poetry collections include *Selected Poems* (2012) and *Mickey Finn's Air* (Gallery 2014). He has also published volumes of essays, most recently, *The Wrong Country* (2018). He is Fellow Emeritus, Trinity College Dublin.

**Julia Deakin** was born in Nuneaton and went north to Yorkshire where she taught, married, did a poetry MA and took up ice-skating. Her collections *The Half-Mile-High Club* – a 2007 Poetry Business Competition winner – *Without a Dog* (Graft, 2008) and *Eleven Wonders* (Graft, 2011) drew praise from nationally renowned poets; her fourth, *Sleepless*, was published by Valley Press last October. She has featured twice on *Poetry Please* and won numerous prizes.

**John F. Deane** was born on Achill Island off the west coast of Ireland. He is founder of Poetry Ireland, and its journal *The Poetry Ireland Review*. He has published many collections of poetry, including *Snow Falling on Chestnut Hill: New & Selected poems*, Carcanet 2012; most recently *Dear Pilgrims*, (Carcanet, 2018), and a 'poetry and faith memoir', *Give Dust a Tongue* (Columba Press, 2015). A collection of poems set on Achill Island with paintings by John Behan, *Achill: The Island* published by Currach Press appeared earlier this year. In 2016 Deane was the Teilhard de Chardin Fellow in Catholic Studies in Loyola University, Chicago and taught a course in poetry.

**Sally Festing**'s fifth collection, *My Darling Derry,* will be published in 2019. Four prizes fed into *Swimming Lessons, Salaams* (Happenstance), *Font,* and *Doors Opening* (Oversteps) which followed journalism, radio plays, academic studies, biographies of Gertrude Jekyll, Barbara Hepworth and other non-fiction books. (www.sallyfesting.info)

**Duncan Fraser** has had poems in the *Agenda* magazine and Online Supplements. Along with Andrew Hadfield he recently prepared an edition of the letters of the great-great-grandson of the poet Edmund Spenser, published by Legenda in April 2017 as *Gentry Life in Georgian Ireland: The Letters of Edmund Spencer (1711-1790)*. He is currently preparing, again with Andrew Hadfield, an edition of Shirley's play *The Politician* for the forthcoming *Oxford Complete Works of James Shirley*.

**John Freeman** taught for many years at Cardiff University and now lives in the Vale of Glamorgan. His most recent books are *What Possessed Me* (Worple Press), and *Strata Smith and the Anthropocene* (Knives Forks and Spoons Press), both published in 2016. Earlier collections include *A Suite for Summer* (Worple), and *White Wings: New and Selected Prose Poems* (Contraband Books). *What Possessed Me* won the Roland Mathias Poetry Award as part of the Wales Book of the Year Awards in November 2017.

**John Gladwell**, who recently died, lived on the North Essex coast and has had poems published in a variety of magazines including *PN Review, The Rialto, Stand, Ambit, London Magazine* and previous issues of *Agenda*.

**Wendy Holborow** born in South Wales, lived in Greece for 14 years where she edited *Poetry Greece*. Her poetry has been published internationally and placed in competitions. She recently gained distinction for a Masters in Creative Writing at Swansea University. Collections include: *After the Silent Phone Call* (Poetry Salzburg, 2015), *Work's Forward Motion* (2016) and *An Italian Afternoon* (Indigo Dreams, 2017) which was a Poetry Book Society Pamphlet Choice Winter 2017/18.

**Simon Tje Jones** is a songwriter/ musician. Originally from the North East, he has lived in London for 30 years and now in Kent. In 2017/18 he has edited and collaborated on a number of poetry/music projects.

**Benjamin Keatinge** (b. 1973) is a Visiting Research Fellow at the School of English, Trinity College Dublin. He has published widely on Irish poetry and is editor of *Making Integral: Critical Essays on Richard Murphy* forthcoming from Cork UP. He taught English literature for nine years at South East European University, Republic of Macedonia. His poetry has previously appeared in *Eborakon*, *Icarus*, *College Green* and *Kore Broadsheets* and he won third prize in the 2017 Red Line Book Festival Poetry Competition for 'Spring, Ballintemple'.

**John Robert Lee** is a Saint Lucian writer. His *Collected Poems 1975-2015* was published by Peepal Tree Press (UK) in 2017

**Merryn MacCarthy** retired to South West France in 2011, and since then has been inspired to write about her experiences, sometimes in French, sometimes in English. A bilingual edition, *Seeking the Mountains*, was published in 2016. Her poems have appeared in *Agenda*, *English* and *The French Literary Review*, and a collection, *Playing Truant*, came out from Agenda Editions in 2010.

**Sue Mackrell**'s poems, short stories, plays and reviews have appeared in a range of publications, most recently in *Agenda*, *Diversifly* (Fairacre Press) and *Please Hear What I'm not Saying*, a Poetry Collaboration for MIND which has been shortlisted for the Saboteur Awards 2018. She works on local history research projects funded by the Heritage Lottery Fund and Heritage England and is keen to give a voice to those in the past who have been silenced including 17th century witches and First World War Conscientious Objectors. She has an MA in Creative Writing from Loughborough University, where she went on to teach.

**Caroline Maldonado** is a poet and translator, living in the UK and Italy. Poetry book publications include *Your call keeps us awake*, co-translations with Allen Prowle of poems by the Italian poet, Rocco Scotellaro (Smokestack books, 2013), a pamphlet, *What they say in Avenale*, (Indigo Dreams Publishing, 2014) and forthcoming, *Isabella* (Smokestack Books, 2019).

**John Matthews** was born in the North of England. He has been an independent scholar and researcher writer since 1980 and has published over a hundred titles including short stories, fiction, and a volume of poetry. He founded and co-edited the literary journal *Labrys*, and has published several poetry pamphlets. He has published in *Temenos Academy Journal* and *Arthuriana* amongst others.

**W S Milne** is a Scotsman living in Surrey. He has worked on *Agenda* for many years, and is a trustee of the magazine. He has just published some Scots poems and stories in the magazine *Lallans*.

**Jessica Mookherjee** has been published widely in print and on-line poetry magazines and anthologies including A*genda, Antiphon, Rialto* and *The North*. She was highly commended for best single poem in the Forward Prize 2017. She has authored two pamphlets, *Swell* (Telltale Press, 2016), *Joyride* (BLeR Press, 2017) and her first full collection, *Flood* (Cultured Llama). Her second collection is *Tigress* (Nine Arches Press, 2019).

**Kim Moore**'s first collection *The Art of Falling* was published by Seren in 2018 and won the Geoffrey Faber Memorial Prize. Her pamphlet *If We Could Speak Like Wolves* was a winner in the 2012 Poetry Business Pamphlet Competition. Her work has been translated into many languages, including Dutch, Macedonian, Polish, Spanish, Norwegian and Croatian. She is a PhD candidate at Manchester Metropolitan University researching poetry and sexism.

**Abegail Morley** was named as one of the five British poets to watch by the *Huffington Post*. She blogs at The Poetry Shed and is co-editor of Against the Grain Poetry Press. She has collections from various publishers including Nine Arches Press.

**Ruth O'Callaghan** has nine collections of poetry, a volume of interviews with internationally famous women poets plus a five poet anthology with Mongolian women poets. Translated into six languages, she has read in countries ranging from Mongolia to USA, is a reviewer, competition adjudicator, mentor and leads workshops both in UK and abroad. She co-organises international poetry festivals, hosts two London poetry venues in London and is the poet for *Strandlines*.

**John O'Donoghue** is the author of *Brunch Poems* (Waterloo Press, 2009); *Fools & Mad* (Waterloo Press, 2014); and *Sectioned: A Life Interrupted* (John Murray, 2009).

**Richard Ormrod** is a published biographer, journalist and poet. His latest book, *Andrew Young, Poet, Priest and Naturalist: A Reassessment*, has recently been published by Lutterworth Press.

**Marie Papier(-Knight)** (who is living in the golden autumn of her age) was born and educated in the French language but has lived in England since the seventies. She has attended four years of London Poetry School, many poetry worshops. She has published three novels, poetry and short stories in French. Some of her poems are published in *The North* and in Arvon/*Daily Telegraph* in English. She attends regular Stanza workshops in Bristol.

**David Pollard** has been furniture salesman, accountant, TEFL teacher and university lecturer. His doctoral thesis was published as: *The Poetry of Keats: Language and Experience*. He has also published *A KWIC Concordance to the Harvard Edition of Keats' Letters*, a novel, *Nietzsche's Footfalls* and six volumes of poetry. Two are ekphrastic, *Self-Portraits* and *Three Artists*. The others are *patricides*, *Risk of Skin*, *bedbound* and *Finis-terre* (from Agenda – a Poetry Book Society choice). He divides his time between Brighton on the South coast of England and a village on the Rias of Galicia.

**Carol Rumens** has published 17+ collections of poetry including, most recently, the chapbook *Bezdelki* (The Emma Press, 2018) which won the 2018 Michael Marks Award, *Animal People* (Seren, 2016), and *Perhaps Bag: Selected Poems* (Sheep Meadow, 2017, USA). Carol also writes fiction and plays and a popular poetry blog for the *Guardian Online*, 'Poem of the Week.' Originally from South London, she currently lives and writes in North Wales.

**Omar Sabbagh** is a widely published poet, writer and critic. His first collection and his latest, fourth collection, are, respectively: *My Only Ever Oedipal Complaint* and *To The Middle of Love* (Cinnamon Press, 2010/17). His Beirut novella, *Via Negativa: A Parable of Exile*, was published with Liquorice Fish Books in March 2016; and a new collection of short fictions, *Dye and Other Stories*, was released in September 2017. He has published or will have published scholarly essays on George Eliot, Ford Madox Ford, G.K. Chesterton, Robert Browning, Henry Miller, Lawrence Durrell, Joseph Conrad, Lytton Strachey, T.S. Eliot, Basil Bunting, Hilaire Belloc, and others; as well as on many contemporary poets.

**Myra Schneider**'s recent collections are *The Door to Colour* (Enitharmon, 2014) and the pamphlet *Persephone in Finsbury Park*, (Second Light Publications, 2016). Other publications include books about personal writing and fiction for young people. She has co-edited poetry anthologies of poetry by contemporary women poets, is consultant to the Second Light Network and a Poetry School tutor. Ward Wood are publishing a new collection *Lifting The Sky* in October 2018.

**Judith Shalan** worked for the BBC in London, for the Arabic Service and Radio Drama, before moving with her family to Kent and then Sussex. She worked as a journalist and subeditor before freelancing which freed her up to do more of her own writing. She has been published by *Agenda* online and in the printed journal.

**Gerard Smyth** has published nine collections, including *A Song of Elsewhere* (Dedalus Press, Dublin 2015), *The Fullness of Time: New and Selected Poems* (Dedalus, 2010 ) and *The Yellow River* (with artwork by Seán McSweeney and published by Solstice Arts Centre, 2017 ). He was the 2012 recipient of the O'Shaughnessy Poetry Award and is co-editor, with Pat Boran, of *If Ever You Go: A Map of Dublin in Poetry and Song* (Dedalus Press) which was Dublin's One City One Book in 2013. He is Poetry Editor of *The Irish Times*.

**Robert Stein**'s first collection *The Very End of Air* appeared in 2011. His poems have been published in *Agenda, Poetry Review, Poetry London, Ambit, The Rialto, Envoi* and elsewhere. 'Mr. Henry F. Talbot's second letter of the day to Miss Alice Thwaites' and 'Birch Trees near Weissenbach, 1907' were both longlisted in the 2017 National Poetry Competition.

**Will Stone** is a poet, essayist and literary translator. He has published three collections of poetry (Salt/ Shearsman). The first, *Glaciation,* won the international Glen Dimplex Award for poetry in 2008. Arc published his *To the Silenced – Selected Poems of Georg Trakl* (2005), *Poems* Emile Verhaeren (2013) and *Poems* Georges Rodenbach (2017). His translation of *Friedrich Hölderlin's Life: Poetry and Madness by Wilhelm Waiblinger* appeared with Hesperus Press in May 2018. Pushkin Press will publish a *Collected Poems* of Georg Trakl in 2019 and *Poems to Night* by Rainer Maria Rilke in 2020.

**Seán Street**'s most recent full collection is *Camera Obscura* (Rockingham Press, 2016). Prose includes his trilogy on sound: *The Poetry of Radio, The Memory of Sound* and *Sound Poetics* (Routledge/Palgrave Macmillan). He is currently writing a fourth in the series, *Sound at the Edge of Perception*, to be published by Palgrave later this year. He is Emeritus Professor at Bournemouth University.

**Siân Thomas** holds a Masters degree in Creative Writing from the University of Sussex and is Poet in Residence for Ashdown Forest. Her work has appeared in various publications, including *Agenda, Poetry Wales, Swamp, The Daily Telegraph, The Rialto* and the anthologies *London Rivers* and *The Needlewriters*. Her first pamphlet *Ovid's Echo* is published by Paekakariki Press and her second *Ashdown* is due this year.

**Shaun Traynor**, Northern Irish poet and children's author; lives in London; his latest collection is *Van Gogh in Brixton* from Muswell Press. See also www.shauntraynor.co.uk

**Marek Urbanowicz** has been published in a number of magazines including *Agenda, Frogmore Papers* and several anthologies. In 2014 he completed an MA in Voice Studies from Royal Central School of Speech and Drama. He is now a qualified voice coach with a special interest in the reading of poetry. He is currently part of the RADA Elders Company. He qualified as an acupuncturist in 1979.

**Judith Wilkinson** is a poet and translator. She has published many collections to date, including Toon Tellegen's *Raptors* (Carcanet, 2011), for which she won the Popescu Prize. Shoestring Press has published two of her own collections, *Tightrope Dancer* (2010) and *Canyon Journey* (2016). She is currently working on a book of 'desert poems', in which she explores the experiences of different people – some real, some imagined – who have spent time in the desert, such as adventurers, artists and recluses.

# W S Milne

## An Eminent Witness of Life

Helen Vendler, in her review of John Crowe Ransom's *Collected Poems*, seems unduly harsh on his poetry (*New York Review of Books*, April 21, 2016). It is hard to see how a poet of his stature can be 'fettered' by technique and by 'the self-conscious irony of his narratives.' For example the lines from 'The Swimmer' which she finds so otiose and ineffective, to my mind magisterially 'reconstitute the world of perceptions' and present 'things as they are in their rich and contingent materiality' (the phrases come from Ransom's second prose book, *The World's Body*) as successfully as any of Keats's *Odes*. They superbly convey the atmosphere of a very hot day, evincing a scene of moral and physical lassitude, a typical Ransom subject. Secondly, she asks why Ransom entitles a poem 'One Who Rejects Christ'. The reason is clear enough. The agonist has no (Calvinistic) sense of Original Sin, of The Fall. He does not realise that there are glories beyond his labour (a theme taken up more brilliantly in 'Antique Harvesters'), the beautiful Edenic Ideal of the Rose (as Dante envisages it at the end of *The Divine Comedy*). Allied to this, she finds *Poems About God* 'a strange title'. Why? Ransom is a Pascalian poet obsessed with metaphysics, hence his most famous critical remark that 'a poem is a desperate ontological manoeuvre'. He summed up his own modern aesthetic by stating categorically (in his essay 'The Tense of Poetry') that 'the plight of a religious poet in an age of reason is desperate'. Professor Vendler goes on to accuse Ransom of 'talking in a language never heard on earth or heaven'. How should God talk, we might ask? Like Milton or Herbert only? Surely not. She adds that the poet 'persists in his quarrel with God'. And why shouldn't he? The whole of Ransom's style (which she finds 'strange' – is it any stranger than Emily Dickinson's or John Berryman's?) lies just there, in his lyrical cry or *ruah*, the rushing of a mighty wind, the Holy Spirit, the creative voice he writes of in his first prose book, *God Without Thunder*. As Geoffrey Hill has perceptively written (in *The Lords of Limit*) 'the idiosyncratic "cry" of a Ransom poem... is simultaneously a "fact" and a resistance to a fact' – of suffering bound up within recalcitrant form.

I cannot for the life of me see why Professor Vendler is so critical of Ransom's most famous poem, 'Bells for John Whiteside's Daughter'. It is surely as chockful of humanity and pathos as Ben Jonson's elegy for his son. In terms of some of the details which confuse her, surely the mourners are 'sternly stopped' by the sight of the dead girl's corpse; the phrase 'her brown study' evocatively suggests death's obscurity (the etymology of the phrase lying in the word 'gloomy') and the girl's lost reverie of innocence; 'primly propped' is just right for the manner in which morticians or undertakers lay out a dead body. 'With ceremony thin as this' (Geoffrey Hill writes in his elegy on Isaac Rosenberg) 'we tidy death'. And so we should. It is a sign of culture and urbanity. As for the geese in the poem, Miller Williams has written (in his book *The Poetry of John Crowe Ransom*) that 'I am at a loss for a reply to any reader who fails to see that the power and the pathos of the scene, the awful reality of the child's death, all live in the geese, the silly, white geese, and that this is consistent with the classic eye Ransom casts on death'. It is of that order of 'heartbreak' which Robert Lowell found (and admired) in the poetry of Thomas Hardy.

Further fault is found with Ransom's supposed 'faux-medievalism' which is supposed to be archaic (in 'Fall of Leaf' especially). 'Dorothy' is argued to be out of place (what are we to make of *The Wizard of Oz*?) and 'Dick' too (what about Dick Diver in *Tender is the Night*?) But surely Ezra Pound is archaic at his modernist best, and so too is Robert Lowell in his magnificent *Lord Weary's Castle*. Are we going to condemn these poets out of hand as 'not to the taste of a contemporary reader'? In addition, Professor Vendler takes umbrage with Ransom's phrase 'a bee in his brain' (likening it to 'a bat in the belfry' – surely the phrase is 'bats in the belfry'?) suggesting eccentricity. To my mind the phrase is employed by Ransom to evince a state of monomania, as in the compound 'wasp-music' in 'Antique Harvesters' – the obsessive crying out upon the constitution of things we find in a typical Ransom poem.

Professor Vendler has an aversion to irony. 'What comes after it?' she asks, and answers 'Nothing: the imagination has been poisoned'. But is this really the case? One has only to think of the work of William Empson to have one's doubts. In point of fact, early on in her review she sets up Auden as a counter to Ransom, but it was Auden himself who wrote of 'the ironic points of light flashing out from the citadels of Justice', meaning that the finest endeavours of the human mind are always compromised by failure and defeat. Herein lies the irony, the humour ('Jesus... tease us') of the human condition, a fact nearly always realised in a Ransom poem.

Finally Professor Vendler takes exception to Ransom's 'death-obsessed poetry', as if 'the cold fury' of science, the 'century of mania' (the phrases are taken from Ransom's prose) had somehow passed her by. 'I go fishing in the dark of my mind' Ransom wrote, and the result is he remains 'an eminent witness of life'. There is nothing 'reductive' that I can see in the poet's supposed 'scheme'. Being is weighed down in the flesh, in the bowels of the world's body, in great poems such as 'Captain Carpenter', 'Painted Head', 'Here Lies a Lady' 'Judith of Bethulia', 'Prelude to an Evening', 'Vision by Sweetwater', and 'Old Mansion'. The world would be a poorer place without them.